SILENT CITIES
SAN FRANCISCO

Also by Jessica Ferri

Silent Cities New York: Hidden Histories of the Region's Cemeteries

SILENT CITIES
SAN FRANCISCO

HIDDEN HISTORIES OF THE REGION'S CEMETERIES

JESSICA FERRI

Globe
Pequot

Guilford, Connecticut

to Roman

Globe Pequot

An imprint of Globe Pequot, the trade division of
The Rowman & Littlefield Publishing Group, Inc.
4501 Forbes Blvd., Ste. 200
Lanham, MD 20706
GlobePequot.com

Distributed by NATIONAL BOOK NETWORK

British Library Cataloguing in Publication Information available

Library of Congress Cataloging-in-Publication Data available

Names: Ferri, Jessica, 1985– author, photographer.
Title: Silent cities San Francisco : hidden histories of the region's cemeteries / Jessica Ferri.
Description: Lanham, MD : Globe Pequot, [2021] | Includes bibliographical references. | Summary: "In 1914, the city of San Francisco exiled its cemeteries, barring burials within city limits and relocating its existing graveyards to the town of Colma, spawning America's only necropolis, where the dead outnumber the living 1000 to 1. This book reveals the complex cultural makeup of the Bay Area, where diversity and history collide, pitting the dead against the living in a race for space and memorialization" — Provided by publisher.
Identifiers: LCCN 2021018788 (print) | LCCN 2021018789 (ebook) | ISBN 9781493056460 (paperback) | ISBN 9781493056477 (epub)
Subjects: LCSH: Cemeteries—California—San Francisco Bay Area—History. | Cemeteries—California—San Francisco—History. | Exhumation—California—San Francisco. | San Francisco Bay Area (Calif.)—History.
Classification: LCC F868.S156 F47 2021 (print) | LCC F868.S156 (ebook) | DDC 979.4/6—dc23
LC record available at https://lccn.loc.gov/2021018788
LC ebook record available at https://lccn.loc.gov/2021018789

♾™ The paper used in this publication meets the minimum requirements of American National Standard for Information Sciences—Permanence of Paper for Printed Library Materials, ANSI/NISO Z39.48-1992.

CONTENTS

Like robes, the elements shall folded lie
In the vast wardrobe of eternity.
—HESTER PULVER, 1648

INTRODUCTION

When I told my friends we were moving to the Bay Area after thirteen years in Brooklyn, most took the news with disbelief and outright disdain. "But you're so New York," seemed to be the feeling. I wasn't thrilled, either. I've never lived on the West Coast and spent most of my time visiting friends in Los Angeles. I don't know San Francisco aside from one trip I took with my family when I was in grade school.

But one friend had a different response. "The Bay Area is so beautiful," she said. "It's really moody. The landscapes—the fog. I think you'll love it there."

I had no idea what she meant. My idea of the San Francisco fog, which locals lovingly refer to as "Karl," came from Alfred Hitchcock's movie *Vertigo*, which was probably created on a soundstage. At the time of the move I was finishing up work on *Silent Cities New York*, a bittersweet but fitting ending to my time there. *Silent Cities San Francisco* wasn't a sure thing yet.

As soon as it did become official, I made my way to Mission Dolores, the oldest cemetery in the region, and to the National Cemetery and the pet cemetery in the Presidio. But I was most excited about visiting Colma, the only necropolis in the United States. It seemed providential that my book would become my introduction to the Bay Area.

Then, just before I could visit Colma for the first time, Covid-19 hit. The Bay Area was one of the first regions to enact a "shelter-in-place" order. My husband started working from home, and my son's daycare closed.

During lockdown, people went to cemeteries in hope of some socially distanced fresh air. I've always encouraged anyone to take advantage of cemeteries' unique offering of history and green space. But some of the cemeteries were so mobbed by crowds unfamiliar with their rules and regulations that they had to close to visitors.

As I write this, some large park cemeteries, like Mountain View, in Oakland, are still closed to the public.

This is not a book about Covid-19, but undoubtedly it affected my research. All the libraries and archives where I would normally do research were closed. Thanks to online databases, I was able to research from afar. Covid-19 has affected us all, globally, and I have a feeling that even with a vaccine we will still be experiencing its influence for years to come. It plays a role in this book, whether I like it or not.

A few months after we moved to San Francisco, and shortly before the outbreak here in the United States, we moved from the city to the East Bay. Instead of being in San Francisco, I was across the bay looking at it. Just a short walk from my house I can see the Bay Bridge, San Francisco, and off in the distance to the right, the Golden Gate Bridge. Well, sometimes I can see this vista. Other days it's completely obscured in fog, totally invisible.

The funny thing about writing a book on the cemeteries of San Francisco is that there are technically no cemeteries in San Francisco. This is not completely true: there are three. There is the cemetery at Mission Dolores, the National San Francisco Cemetery and pet cemetery in the Presidio. That's three. If you count the San Francisco Columbarium (which is more like a mausoleum, not in-ground burial), then there are four that remain. It's not that San Francisco never had many cemeteries. They were all evicted.

Since 1912, not a single person has been buried in San Francisco city limits. As early as the late 1880s cemeteries started to "relocate" out of the city. In 1912, this relocation effort became an official decree—cemeteries were evicted from the city by court order and moved to the town of Colma, about two miles south of Daly City.

Before this lengthy relocation process, there were hundreds of cemeteries in San Francisco, including the "big four": Odd Fellows, Calvary, Masonic, and Laurel Hill. The process of exhuming hundreds of thousands of graves and transporting human remains to Colma was not a pretty or easy task. Most of the dead were reburied in mass graves in different cemeteries in Colma, as the transportation of tombstones and reburial in separate graves was an expense the majority of families could not afford. As decades have passed, and the city of San Francisco has continued to develop, the discovery of hundreds of burials illustrates that the "relocation" to Colma was by no means complete.

When I tell people about the "relocation" process to Colma, most are horrified. Exhuming or moving human remains for any reason is deeply upsetting. The concept of a mass grave is one that most associate with genocide and war. But before modern cities, stolen lands from the native tribes were frequently developed right atop of sacred burial grounds. In the Bay Area, these are called shell mounds. There were over 400 shell mounds at the start of the Gold Rush era in the mid-1800s. Most were demolished by colonizers to build towns, saloons, and pavilions. White people were literally dancing on indigenous graves.

San Francisco's official order of 1912 to prohibit burial and in 1914 to relocate existing burials is not unique. Plenty of cities all over the world have passed similar laws barring burials within city limits or the new construction of cemeteries. But no other city in the United States undertook the effort to relocate the cemeteries like San Francisco. No other city has designated their burial ground to a centralized location like Colma. As a result, the Colma necropolis—literally a city of the dead—is a bizarre wonderland of the history of the people and the development of the Bay Area, all laid together, side by side, in a total of seventeen separate cemeteries.

Colma's existence blurs and obscures the past in San Francisco. Dolores Park, a popular place for tourists and locals alike, is built on top of two of the city's first Jewish cemeteries. The city's first public library, now the Asian Art Museum, the Yerba Buena gardens, and the Legion of Honor, and the adjoining golf course, were all built on land that once belonged to the dead. At Buena Vista Park in Laurel Heights, tombstones that were unclaimed from the big four cemeteries were smashed into pieces and used to line the gutters. Walking along one path, you can still read their epitaphs: "died" "aged 38," "friend."

Many have argued, as the city did in the early 1900s, that the erasure of the past is essential to the progress of the living. During the pandemic, questions over what to do with the dead resurfaced when hospital morgues and funeral homes were unprepared for mass death. No development or progress offers easy answers to how we deal with death, especially on such a mass scale.

One of the first cemeteries we visited in Colma was Cypress Lawn Cemetery. Cypress Lawn is done in the park style and is one of the larger nonsectarian cemeteries. It seemed a good place to start. In reading this book you will notice I refer to "we" instead of "I." Because of Covid restrictions, my husband and I are without childcare. He and my two-year-old son came along to much of the fieldwork I did in writing this book. My son's reaction to what he saw in Colma and all over the Bay Area only added to my experience of these places.

At Cypress Lawn we stumbled upon a gigantic statue seated atop a bench, the Drexler family monument. The sculpture appeared to be a stoic young woman, gazing out over the cemetery. My son asked if he could sit with her on the bench. I snapped about a dozen photos of this striking monument, making a mental note to revisit it in my research.

I am indebted to the work of Michael Svanevik and Shirley Burgett for their book, *City of Souls*, on Colma. In reading that night, I was pleasantly surprised to see a photo of the Drexler memorial we had seen that afternoon. But in the photo in *City of Souls*, the sculpture was different. She had wings, and held a sword! It turns out she wasn't a she at all, but rather the Archangel Michael. The wings and sword had been badly damaged during

the 1906 earthquake, and while the statue was repaired, they were never reattached. The monument still stands, but its symbolism is missing.

The presence of a cemetery anywhere is proof of what came before: the kind of people, where they came from, what they died of, and lessons we can learn from them. When that cemetery disappears from view, so does our awareness of the past. As with the statue in Cypress Lawn, misunderstanding and confusion ensue.

In the Bay Area, there is a thick fog on early mornings that usually dissipates before breakfast. Some days it doesn't lift. As a New Yorker, I like the fog. It doesn't seem like bad weather compared to dirty snow or freezing rain. But in that thick fog the entire city disappears. Though I know San Francisco is there, when the sun burns through, it's a relief to see it still stands.

PART I

SAN FRANCISCO

THE FAILED STAR

THE MISSION

Shot on location in San Francisco, Alfred Hitchcock's *Vertigo* tells the story of ex-cop Scottie (suffering from vertigo after he witnesses his partner fall to his death) who is approached by an old friend named Gavin Elster who asks him to follow his wife, Madeleine, who has been acting strangely. Scottie can't deny the impulse to get back into detective work, so he gamely follows

Madeleine around San Francisco, eventually saving her life and falling in love with her in the process.

Vertigo is appreciated for its early special effects, the dolly zoom camera trick sometimes called "the vertigo effect," and the fact that large parts of the movie progress without any dialogue: the scenes where Scottie follows Madeleine in his car, undetected, with Bernard Herrmann's fantastic musical score. Film buffs have made a small tourist industry out of visiting the locations in the movie, most of which can still be seen today.

During her day out, Madeleine visits Mission Dolores, the oldest structure in San Francisco. Founded in 1774, the mission includes the small original building and an adjoining, larger addition, the Basilica, built in 1918 with a redesign in 1926. The "mission" was to convert as many people to Catholicism, but, as we well know, in addition to destroying native culture, the missions also destroyed the native people. To the side of the original building there is a cemetery, "the final resting place for numerous Ohlone, Miwok, and other First Californians as well as notable California pioneers," according to the Mission Dolores website, "the only cemetery that remains within city limits." This is nearly true.

In the film, Scottie follows Madeleine several steps behind her (remember he is secretly following her) while Herrmann's strings sing sweetly, into the church and out to the cemetery where she walks to the front of the cemetery gate and stops for several minutes to pay her respects to one tombstone in particular. In Hitchcock's glowing soft filter, he waits for her to move on before he approaches the stone, notepad in hand, to see the person to which it belongs. The name floods the screen as the mission bells chime and the score takes an ominous tone:

CARLOTTA VALDES
born
December 3, 1834
died
March 5, 1857

I went looking for Carlotta Valdes on my first Halloween in San Francisco. If I hadn't been so overwhelmed by my recent move to New York, I might have planned a Madeleine costume. Based on what I had on hand, I decided to go as Lydia Deetz from *Beetlejuice*, despite the fact that I know no one in San Francisco and had no Halloween party plans. Needless to say I got some weird looks riding the streetcar to Mission Dolores. The staff in the gift shop, though, were unfazed.

"Searching for Carlotta Valdes," I wrote in the caption of one of my Instagram posts from the day. "I hope you find Carlotta," responded one of my followers.

There is a small box for donations before you enter the original mission. Built to honor St. Francis of Assisi, it features a stunning altar, priceless paintings of the Virgin and child, and tombs underfoot. Outside the side door, there are dioramas of what the original mission looked like, and a small alley that leads to the gorgeous, domed Basilica.

Being Halloween, the Basilica was all decked out for Dia de los Muertos, with a spectacular altar depicting the crucifixion. The bright paper flowers matched the colors in the enormous stained glass window above this corner, bathing the entire sanctuary in bright pink light. At the foot of Christ, there were painted skulls and portraits of the deceased, along with candles and offerings, like a bottle of Mexican Coca-Cola. As I made my way to the front of the church, I realized I was not alone. There were two men, deep in prayer, in the front left pew. I quickly snapped a few photos and made myself scarce. I wanted to get to the cemetery.

Through a side entrance, you enter the cemetery at the back of the mission. It hasn't changed much since Hitchcock filmed here in 1958. It was a gorgeous day with bright blue skies. It feels like a private courtyard, with the tall, thin slate stones giving it away as a cemetery, and the statue of Junipero Serra standing centrally, head bowed, lost in thought.

I was alone for most of the time I walked through the paths, until two ladies, obviously tourists, came through and snapped a few photos. I felt a bit like Scottie, trying to keep my distance and give them space.

Most of the markers, made of slate, stone, or marble, are the graves of Europeans who immigrated to California in the 1800s. The graves line the borders of the mission's property, right up to a plain metal fence that separates them from an alleyway and the back of several houses. The grave of a child who died in 1859, at

seven years, three months, and twenty-one days, is a reminder of the rough conditions of early California, even for the wealthy. His family includes this moving epitaph:

The last and sad gift
Which a Mothers Love can Bestow
Upon his Mortal Remains
Calmly Sleeping here

As I stopped to think on the loss of this child, the only sound in the cemetery was the sound of laughing children. I walked toward the back of the land and discovered that there is now a school right alongside the back of the mission, with a playground directly opposite the fence.

Near the statue of Junipero Serra there is a wooden double tombstone for two people, presumably a couple, with their dates and also the dates on which they were baptized. The wooden

marker is obviously new, as their death dates are in the early 1800s, any marker would have obviously degraded over time. Their presence, near the statue of Serra, is a reminder that this mission is a church—founded here with the express purpose of converting native people to Catholicism.

The statue of Junipero Serra is one that rather eerily anticipates his complicated legacy. He stands on a pedestal, in the cloak of a Franciscan, wearing a rosary around his neck. His head is bowed, presumably in prayer, with his arms tucked behind his back. He looks down, fatigued, at his sandaled feet.

All over San Francisco you'll find Junipero Serra, in the names of streets, buildings, and other civic places. Serra was born in 1713 in Majorca, Spain, and and in 1749, landed in Mexico with the distinct goal of founding a ministry in the new world. By 1767, Serra had made it to Baja, California. The plaque that adorns his statue at Mission Dolores reads: Junipero Serra O.F.M, Founder and First President of the California Missions.

Serra died in 1784 and was beatified by Pope John Paul II in 1988, and canonized by Pope Francis in 2015. But his sainthood is controversial. Serra's conversion methods were dramatic and often violent. Since his canonization, statues of Serra all over California have been toppled. As recently as June 2020, a statue of Serra in San Francisco's Golden Gate Park was torn down and covered in red paint.

Carlotta's character is part of a ruse—spoilers abound—Madeleine is supposedly possessed by the spirit of Carlotta, her great-grandmother, who committed suicide after she bore a child by a married man. Gavin has conspired with his mistress Judy to murder the real Madeleine and have Judy, pretending to be Madeleine, convince Scottie that she is suicidal. Because of his vertigo, Elster knows Scottie won't be able to climb the tower at San Juan Batista to stop her. Judy, as Madeleine, runs up to the top of the tower as Elster throws the lifeless body of his murdered wife from the top instead. Scottie, overcome with vertigo, is helpless to stop her.

I didn't find a tombstone for Carlotta Valdes at Mission Dolores because Carlotta Valdes isn't real, of course, though her stone, a prop left by the *Vertigo* crew, did remain in the graveyard for some time. To exit the cemetery, you walk back through the gift shop where you entered. There are rosaries, religious icons, Mexican skulls, candles, and other Catholic wares for sale, all which go toward keeping the mission in good shape. It is still an active

church. On the back wall there is a portrait of Hitchcock filming at Mission Dolores.

The mission served as a film set, but it is real. Its facade has remained the same for hundreds of years, but additions and repairs have been made. That a structure could be so old contributes to a feeling of disbelief, that there must be artifice at work. Just a short walk down the sidewalk from Mission Dolores is Dolores Park, a

popular park for picnics and lounging with a large playground at the top of its hill.

Before Dolores Park was Dolores Park, it was two of the largest and oldest Jewish cemeteries in San Francisco. At their borders were a few other Catholic cemeteries, located near the mission. A great deal of the entire Mission district was made up of cemeteries.

You would never know this after spending a day at Dolores Park. There are no markers, no plaques or other civic indicators that this land was once filled with graves.

Without a doubt, the two events that contributed to the making of modern San Francisco are the Gold Rush of 1850 and the 1906 earthquake. "A village of five or six hundred people in early

1848, San Francisco was a city of twenty-five thousand by the end of 1849," Charles Wollenberg writes in *Berkeley: A City in History*. And by the time California was granted statehood in 1850, "it already had the most diverse population of any American state."

The Gold Rush brought thousands of Americans and immigrants hoping, if not for gold, than for a new life in the West. Cemeteries were created as needed in San Francisco as the city expanded. Different groups, based on religion, then nonsectarian cemeteries, popped up all over San Francisco. But California was new to the cemetery business—new to statehood, in fact, and few of these graveyards were planned with "endowment care," or "perpetual care," ensuring their upkeep for the future.

By the late 1800s the cemeteries had become neglected and overgrown as most of the dead's families, if they had any, had died themselves or moved on. With no funds to take care of the cemeteries, they became vulnerable. Mission Dolores had been designated a historic place, and the fact that it was still an active church

OPENSFHISTORY.ORG

protected its cemetery from neglect and vandalism. But as early as 1880, the city was eager to remove the cemeteries and develop their land, approximately 162 acres, or 60 to 70 blocks in the center of San Francisco.

The 1906 earthquake was the nail in the San Francisco cemeteries' coffin. The damage that the cemeteries suffered as a result of the earthquake only made it easier for thieves to steal from the dead. The cemeteries became dangerous places. Germ theory was still a new concept in the late 1800s. All of this, combined with the smell from recently desecrated graves, made a compelling argument for the city to "do something" about the cemeteries.

But you can't simply get rid of cemeteries, so, first, the city passed a law prohibiting any burials within city limits. Anticipating what was to come, the Catholic cemeteries at Dolores Park recognized they needed to move. Holy Cross Cemetery was founded in Colma, in 1887. The two Jewish cemeteries where Dolores Park now stands followed suit. For the cemeteries left in the city, this only made matters worse. Now with no funds from burials, they had even less to keep up the grounds.

OPENSFHISTORY.ORG

SAN FRANCISCO HISTORY CENTER, SAN FRANCISCO PUBLIC LIBRARY

An article from *San Francisco News* on June 30, 1939, reads like the opening of the "Thriller" music video read by Vincent Price: "On moonless, foggy nights, shadowy forms have slunk into vaults. Clanking sounds, the muffled crash of a sledge-hammer, have echoed forth as vandals looted the vaults of bronze flower urns, of silver coffin handles."

Under normal circumstances, we would have been frequent visitors to Dolores Park. I love its proximity to Mission Dolores, my son loves the playground. But with Covid, we avoided going into San Francisco unless it was absolutely necessary. One night, because of severe weather in the East Bay, we had to evacuate and spent one night in a hotel in the city. Since cases were down in the Bay Area, we thought we'd take a trip to the playground at Dolores Park.

As soon as we pulled up, I regretted this decision. The park was swarmed with people. "I don't like this," I said to my husband, "it's too crowded." He assured me that we were only heading to the playground, which was less well-attended, and that we'd be outside wearing masks. I reluctantly went along. As we walked through the park (the only way to get to the playground, which is at the base of a steep, muddy hill), there were people in varying states of intoxication. Men were lined up at the MUNI station, taking turns peeing in a small gazebo that I suppose gave them some sort of semblance of privacy.

Judging from the behavior of the crowds, it was obvious that quarantine had taken its toll. As we walked past the hordes of people, I realized the cops were following closely behind us, handing out face masks wrapped in plastic to those not wearing masks. I didn't see anyone refuse one, but most people just took them and put them in their pockets, not on their face.

The playground was less crowded than the park itself but that wasn't saying much. Kids ran amok—jumping over each other to get to the top of the slide, clambering up the side rather than using the stairs. There were several collisions at the bottom. Parents ran after their younger children, pulling up their face masks. Older kids weren't wearing masks at all. I watched as a little girl sneezed, wiped her nose, and then went to play with a set of drums. At least five other kids immediately followed her, dirtying their hands.

"Did you know this whole place used to be a cemetery?" I said to my husband, hoping to ground my anxiety in some kind of irony that felt comforting. "Really?" he said. "Yeah, Jewish cemeteries," I appealed. "There are too many people here," I repeated. "But we're outside," he said, "it's safe."

I thought back to the way the San Francisco cemeteries must have looked after years of neglect. Not only were they an eye-sore, but according to *City of Souls*, the community was worried about "invisible effluvia" from the dead bodies, particularly those who had died of disease, would infect "little children and wives." Needless to say, standing in Dolores Park playground just as Covid-19 restrictions were being relaxed, thinking of "invisible effluvia" did not help to ease my anxiety. By this time, it had reached what I might categorize as panic.

Walking back to the car, I questioned my motives. Why had I gone along with the trip to the playground when I didn't think it was safe? Why was the park so crowded with people when we were all supposed to avoid crowds? Why were some people not wearing masks?

Covid-19 is unseen. Invisibility makes things more dangerous. Thinking of the cemeteries that had stood directly there, I imagined the difficult work of removing the bodies. In 1950, the city commissioned a report on the relocation process, published as "Location, Regulation, and Removal of Cemeteries in the City and County of San Francisco," revealing details of the work. When Laurel Hill was exhumed, a total of 35,000 bodies were moved to Colma, a process that took sixteen months. "The view of curious passers-by was screened by six-foot cloth windscreens," the report's author, William A. Proctor, writes. At Calvary, the Catholic cemetery, "screens were erected to prevent intrusion of curious onlookers, and work was carried on in an 'careful and reverent manner.'"

When I tell people about the fact that nearly 130,000 bodies from San Francisco's cemeteries were dug up and moved to Colma, the most common reaction I get is one of shock and disgust. And yet, in this 1950 report, Proctor describes "curious passers-by" and the "intrusion of curious onlookers," desperate to see.

Jacqueline Rose, in writing about Freud and our response to the Covid-19 pandemic in an essay for the *London Review of Books*, raises the important lessons of the flu pandemic of 1918. The flu, which killed approximately 675,000 Americans and still kills about 34,000 each year, "has turned out to be a silent stalker of history, barely included in lists of the world's modern afflictions, even though its death toll came close to the combined toll of the two world wars. Laura Spinney—whose book about the Spanish flu, *Pale Rider*, was published before the arrival of Covid-19— suggests that what can fairly be described as the worst 'massacre' of the 20th century has been rubbed out of history."

When the cemeteries were moved to Colma, they were also erased from memory, or, at least, removed. Most who live in San Francisco have no idea they ever existed, much less the tourists who visit the city. Most Americans have never heard of Colma, or know that it is a necropolis, a planned city of the dead. No one knew that many bodies had been left behind until 1950, "when we put up our first major building after the depression," Alan Ziajka, the University of San Francisco's official historian, told KQED. "That was the

Gleeson Library . . . what was once the Masonic Cemetery. At least 200 bodies were found during excavations, when a backhoe turned up a whole mausoleum . . . since then, every time a major excavation has occurred on campus, remains have been found."

If you try and find the locations of the "Big Four" cemeteries in San Francisco, you will find the University of San Francisco, whose Laurel Heights campus is built directly atop where they once stood. You will find a shopping mall with a Trader Joe's and a Target. There is no sign anywhere indicating that this area was once a graveyard.

In *Imperial San Francisco*, Gray Brechin writes that "cities are humanity's most complex artifacts." In service of the need for growth, for development, for land—the rabid spirit of expansion of the West—San Francisco sacrificed its past. And yet, "for all the imperial pretensions of its leaders, San Francisco's population has never exceeded eight hundred thousand nor, since 1856, a land area more than forty-seven square miles—meager by comparison with New York or London."

For those of us interested in the service cemeteries provide to history, there is a kind of cognitive dissonance in San Francisco, a feeling that something is off. But for many the thought of death and dying is pushed back so far into a small corner in their brain that the fact that there no cemeteries in the city doesn't even occur to them. They are completely invisible, physically and psychically.

At the end of *Vertigo*, following Madeleine's death, Scottie sees a woman on the streets of San Francisco who looks just like her, but different. Madeleine was a severe ice blonde. Judy is voluptuous and brunette. Despite the fact that they are clearly not the same person, Scottie not only pursues Judy, but refashions her into the form of Madeleine, making her wear the same suit, the same shoes, changing her makeup, and finally her hair. When this horrifying Pygmalion emerges from the bathroom at the hotel where she lives, bathed in an eerie green light, Scottie knows, and we know, it is Madeleine. We can see her now.

Though Madeleine is supposed to be dead, erased—she still exists in Scottie's mind, and he is determined to make her live again. Only by bringing her back to life can he be redeemed.

Like my willingness to enter Dolores Park when it was clearly overcrowded, the denial of disaster and death only speaks to its intensity. "Truth, they say, is the first casualty of war; but psychic truth is not what is being talked about here," Rose writes. "War and pandemic strip the mind bare. They share a brute ability to smother our psychic repertoire."

I had wanted to believe it was safe. I so desperately wanted to take a walk through Dolores Park, to take my son to the playground that he loves, that I had spontaneous amnesia over the pandemic. As soon as we'd left the park it all came flooding back. San Francisco is missing an enormous chunk of its essential history, but the removal of the cemeteries cannot erase their influence on the city. As much as we try, we cannot exile death.

THE GLORIOUS DEAD

As cemeteries were being evicted from the rest of the city, in addition to Mission Dolores, another group was deemed important enough to remain: the military cemetery.

San Francisco National Cemetery is located in the Presidio, a military fort that was first founded by the Spanish in 1776. Since then it has passed from Spanish to Mexican control, and then, as a result of the Mexican American War and California's statehood in 1850, the American military.

As Gray Brechin puts it in *Imperial San Francisco*, "the real object of the revolution" leading up to the Mexican American War "was to get San Francisco Bay." The Presidio became the most important military post of the West, looking out the Pacific Ocean toward Asia.

In the postwar period, the Presidio's importance to the US military operations became less essential, and in 1972 it was included as part of the Golden Gate Recreation Area. In 1994 it came under the protection of the National Park Service. Today, it is a gigantic, gorgeous park with stunning views of Alcatraz and the Golden Gate Bridge. You can live in the Presidio, in homes that once belonged to military families, and some of the buildings have even been repurposed for small businesses.

For purposes of clarification, there are only four remaining "cemeteries" in San Francisco: Mission Dolores, San Francisco National, the Pet Cemetery of the Presidio, and the San Francisco Columbarium. Though, under a stringent definition of the term, the pet cemetery and the columbarium, a structure that houses cremains, are not technically cemeteries.

That Mission Dolores and the National Cemetery remain in the city speaks to the power and influence of religion and the military in San Francisco.

It took me about two months to get settled in San Francisco before I finally made it out to the National Cemetery in the Presidio. I reveled in the beautiful architecture of the "painted ladies," the Victorian row houses that San Francisco is famous for, as we drove through Pacific Heights. As we entered Golden Gate Park, its beauty was undeniable. Large redwoods stand guard at its entrance, and the farther you drive in, the closer you get to the bay, with sweeping views and plenty of sidewalks.

I arrived at the front gate of the cemetery. It was a crisp January morning; there were no clouds in the bright blue sky, and very little fog. I hadn't realized I would be so close to the bridge. As I

walked up the path toward the cemetery office, the Gate emerged from behind the trees. The office appeared to be closed, and there was a sign about coyotes.

It felt great to be back in the field after a long period away. As I walked up the pathway, the cemetery unfolded in the neat, white rows typical of military cemeteries. It was much larger than I expected. I turned around to face the bay and there was Alcatraz.

As most of my New York expat friends have decamped to Los Angeles, Northern California has remained a bit of a mystery to me. San Francisco's downtown does not come close to competing with New York City. But, once you make your way to the margins of the city and see Golden Gate Park, the natural beauty is stupendous. New York is attractive in its own way—it is undoubtedly glamorous. Northern California's beauty is something different. It is a natural beauty. The gigantic cypress trees, set against the blue sky and the burnt orange of the Golden Gate Bridge: it is almost laughable. It makes you ask, "are you joking?"

Military cemeteries are a form of fearful symmetry. Their perfect lines and uniform stones are meant to promote a sense of peace and equality in death. I often find them to be overwhelming. The endless number and overarching sameness removes a sense of the individual loss. But this is what military service is about, or supposed to be about: sacrifice for the greater good. In his excellent book about visiting the cemeteries of World War I in France, *The Missing of the Somme*, Geoff Dyer remarks that they are memorials not to "our" glorious dead but "the" glorious dead—as if death makes the dead one equal group, and absolves us of any responsibility in their demise.

Shortly after the US military assumed control of the Presidio in 1846, the National Cemetery was established here, meaning that its veterans range from the Civil War and beyond, dwindling around the time San Francisco began the relocation process of its cemeteries. According to its website, the first "American" burial took place in 1854, and after it was formally recognized by the

government in 1884, it became the first National Cemetery on the West Coast.

The day I visited the cemetery there was not a single other person in attendance. The grounds were completely empty of living people. On a central flagpole, the Stars and Stripes whipped in the breeze. One statue to my right was dedicated to the Navy. On the side of the pedestal facing the sun there was a gorgeous carving of a steamship. A sculpture of a soldier, sword drawn, flag bared, stood atop the statue, staring intently over the bay.

Up the path was a stately tombstone, larger than the others, for Arthur Cranston, "killed in action with Modoc Indians in the

Lava Beds, California, April 26, 1873." His epitaph reads: "Greater love hath no man than this, a man lay down his life for his friends."

I had never heard of the Modoc War. In 1872, after a resistance to invasion in which fifty-three Modoc warriors held off three thousand American troops for months at the Lava Beds, the military sent a peace mission to the Modoc native people of

Northern California and Oregon in 1873. Hoping to send a message that they would not surrender, they killed a general and a reverend, and the military responded with more force, eventually capturing the Modoc leader Kintpuash, known as Captain Jack. Presumably, Arthur Cranston must have been killed in one of the battles with the Modoc.

Kintpuash was betrayed by two members of his tribe, who worked with the government to get him to surrender, assuring him that that they would be able to remain on their land. But once he was brought in, Kintpuash was charged with war crimes and executed alongside three of his warriors. Their severed heads were sent to the Army Medical Museum for research, and the remaining Modoc were sent to Oklahoma, where they were held as prisoners of war on a reservation until 1909. Afterward, some returned to Oregon, and others stayed in Oklahoma. About 200 Modoc directly descended from Kintpuash live on the Oklahoma reservation today. When his descendants discovered that his skull had been transferred to the Smithsonian, they requested its return and those of the three warriors who had been executed with him. In 1984 the skulls were returned to the Modoc. The name Kintpuash means "strikes the water brashly."

A few rows behind Arthur Cranston, I found David Lee Hyde, a young man who was killed in action in Korea at the age of twenty-four and received the Purple Heart. Just across from his stone there laid a wreath on another, its greenery dead but the bright red bow sticking out like a blooming rose.

One of the most famous people buried at San Francisco National is Pauline Fryer, a woman who worked as a spy for the Union during the Civil War. Pauline Cushman was a Southern actress who used her popularity among the Confederate soldiers to listen in on their plans for battle. She was eventually captured by the Rebels and scheduled to be executed but used her acting chops to pretend she was ill. The execution was postponed, and Pauline survived.

She was made an honorary major by Abraham Lincoln. But in the years after the war she suffered from a number of tragedies, including the death of her young children, divorce, and widowhood. Eventually coming to San Francisco, she died here at the age of sixty, alone and destitute, most likely a suicide. She was buried at the San Francisco National Cemetery with full military honors. Her simple white stone reads simply: "Pauline C. Fryer, Union Spy."

Toward the back of the cemetery a large black slab popped out among the small white stones. This is the resting place of Phillip and Sala Burton. Phillip Burton was a California congressman who was instrumental in the creation of Golden Gate Park and supported essential medical research at the height of the AIDS crisis. When he died of an aortic aneurysm at age fifty-six, his wife Sala won a special election to serve out his term and was reelected for two more terms. When Sala died at age sixty-one of colon cancer in 1987, Nancy Pelosi won the Burtons' seat and eventually became the first female Speaker of the House.

Sala's epitaph is one of my all-time favorites: "One must care about a world one will not see. She cared."

Just around the curve from the Burtons' grave is the back fence of the cemetery, dwarfed by hundreds of impossibly tall eucalyptus trees. Three graves stood out near the back wall, all veterans of the Spanish American War. Two had a date of death separated by two weeks. I turned to look back at the rest of the cemetery, the sweeping lines of white tombs like poised dominoes, half in shade, half in the brilliant sun.

Coming out from the other side of the slope, I was at the bottom of the hill, surrounded on both sides by regimented white stones, all the same, no outliers. Practically any angle I took with my camera revealed more and more tombstones. I attempted to imagine each of them as individuals, with lives, families, passions. Paying attention to each stone I realized that some—many, in fact—had the name and epitaph of another person on the back. There was a pattern: the deceased veteran on the front of the tombstone, their wives on the back.

Mary, Beatrice, Catherine. His Wife Hazel. His Wife Augusta. I love reading the names: Lulu, Grace Darling. Some of the women were veterans themselves. Newer stones were not always a wife, but instead a child: Their Son. Most of these were infants: 1961–1961.

I made my way down the path back toward the front of the cemetery. The shade from the cypress trees made for incredible lighting. The stones stood watching as I could not stop taking photographs. There was still moisture in the air, making it look as if the cemetery was bathed in an eerie mist.

Near the front gate, the Golden Gate Bridge stood in the distance. Among the uniform stones there were two pedestals, one with a little statue of a soldier, clasping the flag. This is the memorial of Thomas Thompson, who was killed in action, aged twenty, during the Battle of Caloocan during the Philippines-American War in 1899. His parents, Nels and Mary, commissioned the statue, and theirs is the pedestal directly next to him. After the details of his death, his epitaph reads: "Sleep on brave Tommy, and take thy rest / God took thee home when he thought best."

I was closing out my time at San Francisco National Cemetery, but there was one more cemetery I needed to see before I could call it quits for the day. Following directions from Google Maps on foot, I exited the cemetery and took a right. I walked for about ten minutes, coming to a large open field before realizing I had walked in the completely wrong direction. I doubled back, passed the cemetery again, and this time walked the right way, toward the Golden Gate Bridge.

As I passed the cemetery, now on the other side of the street, I saw several people peeking through the gates and taking photos from the sidewalk. I wanted to tell them, the cemetery is open! Why don't you just go inside?

I turned off the main road onto a narrow dirt path that took me down an area shaded with trees. There was one other man traversing the same path who appeared to be hiking. I looked down the slope, and there was nothing but abandoned-looking buildings. Frustrated that I had gone in the wrong direction again, I thought about asking someone for help, but there was no one to ask.

Finally, I rounded the corner and noticed the highway—this was a good sign, because I knew the cemetery was located underneath the freeway overpass. As I got closer, I could see a gate and an open clearing. I had arrived at the Presidio Pet Cemetery.

About 2,000 military families lived in the Presidio when the cemetery was founded in 1952. The pet cemetery was created out of a need for a burial for their pets, and nearly full by 1963, officially

barring burials in 1998. The gigantic pillars that hold up the freeway make the already small cemetery look even smaller. And the little markers, many of them made out of makeshift materials, give it a sad atmosphere.

A family of four passed by as I was standing by the fence taking photographs of the entrance to the cemetery. The children seemed old enough to be interested in the cemetery, and I wondered if they would stop to take a look. But when I looked over to greet them, the mother gave me a suspicious hello, grabbed her son by the hand, and continued on. Her husband looked over at the sign with a quizzical look as they walked by.

A sign at the front of the cemetery indicates that the Presidio Trust has undertaken a "renovation" of the grounds. Given its age and its location, though, I thought it was looking pretty good.

Pet cemeteries are some of the most sentimental places on earth. Only the most miserly person feels nothing in a pet cemetery. Pets are people too, of course, and they play such an important role in our lives, teaching us about compassion and caregiving,

giving more than they can receive, providing unconditional comfort and emotional support.

The names (Button, Judy, Pepper) and epitaphs in a pet cemetery are always what get me. Only in a pet cemetery can we wit-
ness unadulterated, untempered mourning. Some of the markers
have a sense of humor that captures our relationship with our pets.
The first one I read upon entering: "Our Knuckle Head: Parakeet
to Paradise."

There was no one else visiting the cemetery when I was there,
though it has a cult following in guidebooks about cemeteries and
by locals. When I first moved to the East Bay, nearly everyone I
told about this book asked me if I had seen the pet cemetery in the
Presidio. It is obvious that pet cemeteries allow us to have a freer
discourse about death.

The crafty nature of the markers at this cemetery only adds to
the heart-wrenching experience of the place. One can imagine a
family making a wooden marker for their beloved dog, asking the
children, "What should we write about Sadie?" "Just put, she was

a good dog." Well said. For Rusty, who was born in fall 1962 and died in spring 1972, "Greatest dog in the world. He will never be forgotten."

"Charlie was my favorite pet I ever had. He was my bird."

"Mr. Twister: He will be in my <3 where ever he goes my #one-derful little man in Basset clothes, Ken."

"Trouble: He was no trouble."

"Louise: Beloved rat, friend."

San Francisco National Cemetery and the Pet Cemetery are inextricably linked by their location in the Presidio. The Pet Cemetery is a military cemetery by association, due to the fact that most of these pets belonged to the military families who lived here. Undoubtedly they provided love, support, and stability for the children who probably moved often, or experienced long periods without one of their parents. If the cemetery was founded in 1952, then the families here would have lived through the immediate

aftermath of World War II, the Korean War, the Vietnam War, and other conflicts. These pets performed an important service back home as their owners served overseas.

Exiting the Pet Cemetery, I continued down the path leading to the waterfront. There was a massive open green space just below the Golden Gate Bridge. It had become a bit chilly, so it was sparsely attended. In the distance, I could see Alcatraz.

Being the morbid little kid that I was and still am, I was obsessed with Alcatraz as soon as I learned what it was. I visited the island and took the infamous tour with my parents when I was about ten. I don't remember much aside from the graffiti on the outside that remained from the occupation by indigenous activists, the library, and the tour guide closing us in a cell and locking the door. That was really thrilling.

The story of Alcatraz is unsurprisingly a mini-version of the story of San Francisco and the Bay Area itself. Once it belonged to the Spanish, then the Mexicans, always used as a fort and defense against would-be invaders. Then it belonged to the United States, and was used much in the same manner, in defense of the bay and then as storage for munitions the military didn't want the Confederates to get their hands on during the Civil War. It became a military prison, and then, in 1934, the notorious federal penitentiary. Like the Presidio, it now belongs to the National Park Service.

People who died on Alcatraz were sent to Angel Island, two miles away. Also a military post, Fort McDowell, Angel Island was used as a quarantine station for returning troops, and then an immigration center. Like Alcatraz, it is now a state park. Across from the chapel there was a small cemetery, with approximately 143 burials, about a fourth of them coming from Alcatraz. Others were children who died on the island, or unclaimed bodies from the bay of people who had most likely died as a result of violence. When the military relinquished control of the island in 1947, they took the dead with them. Remains were exhumed and moved to Golden Gate National Cemetery in San Bruno.

Golden Gate National Cemetery was established in 1937 as the new military cemetery once burials had ceased in San Francisco proper and the "relocation" of the nonmilitary cemeteries was nearly completed. After expanding its land many times, San Francisco National had become mostly full, and although family members can still be buried in an existing plot, it was closed to new interments. Burials began at Golden Gate Cemetery in 1941.

With incredible views of the San Bruno mountains, Golden Gate Cemetery is well worth a visit. Because the cemetery is newer than San Francisco National, in addition to wives on the back of stones, you will see many more children, and other family members, brothers, friends.

Alcatraz could not have a cemetery itself because the ground is solid rock. It still stands as a menacing sentinel in the distance, the prison to end all prisons. It once held some of the most notorious

criminals in American history, housed there, no doubt, because of its intimidating island location. The threat was that even if you escaped it was only an escape to certain death in the icy-cold, "shark-infested" waters of the bay.

Shark attacks in the bay are extremely rare. Most escapees were captured or shot, but few drowned. Today, people compete in the Escape from Alcatraz Triathlon, of which the swim is only a fraction of the course. But the event takes place in June, when waters are warmest, and presumably, they compete in wetsuits. Gazing at Alcatraz in the distance, I contemplated making an escape in total darkness, at the mercy of the temperature of the bay waters. But there were several who potentially made it to shore, a distance of 1.5 miles. Their fate remains unknown.

THIS PARTICULAR DEATH
WAS NOT INEVITABLE

I don't remember when I first learned about AIDS. But I do remember the first time I came in contact with its horror. Long before I knew the names of the artists David Wojnarowicz or Peter Hujar, I saw the photographs Wojnarowicz took of Hujar just minutes after his death from AIDS in 1987. If memory serves me right, I think I saw them in a documentary, meaning they flashed across the screen before I could truly look at them. That fleeting image stayed in my mind, unattached to its artist or subject, for years.

Shortly after my son was born, I read David Wojnarowicz's *Close to the Knives*. It was good timing; the Whitney Museum in New York was planning a retrospective of his work. I was determined to go and I wanted to attend during the week so that the museum would be less crowded. I strapped my son to my body in his baby carrier and made the journey into the city.

More familiar with Wojnarowicz's photographs, I was stunned by the large-scale paintings he had done. Eventually I came to the room and the piece that I hoped would be included, the photographs of Hujar. There are three of them, one of his hands, his feet, and then his head and face. Looking back at my day at the museum in the photos I took with my phone, there are several selfies of my son and I, and images of the artwork. But I couldn't bring myself to photograph the portraits of Hujar. It felt invasive. I simply stood there for several minutes, taking them in, grateful that they were immobilized, pinned to the wall, where I could really look at them.

My son got antsy and was desperate to get out of the carrier. The exhibit was not crowded so I asked the security guard if he minded if he crawled around. "That's fine," he said, "as long as he doesn't touch the artwork." A few people drifted in and out of the room while he crawled near me on the bench. My back aching, relieved to be free of the weight, I sat there for some time before suiting up again and heading toward the exit.

An older man stopped us on our way toward the elevator. "A very young museumgoer!" he exclaimed, "And what does he think of the art?" He paused, waiting, as if my son would respond. "I think he likes it!" I said, stupidly. "What did you think of the art?" he asked me directly. "Powerful . . ." I stammered. "Disturbing," I clarified. "A big show for a little person," he said, with the hint of judgment in his tone.

Close to the Knives is an intense read, particularly for its ability to communicate what it was like for Wojnarowicz to watch all his friends die, only to become sick himself, while the US government did nothing, only making it more difficult for people to get treatment or adequate medical care for what they called a "gay cancer."

When I was in grade school, AIDS was always referred to as "the AIDS epidemic." Since 1981, when the disease was first given a name, about 700,000 Americans have died of AIDS. Even with advancements in drugs and treatment, about 13,000 Americans still die of AIDS each year. Nearly one million people die of AIDS worldwide each year. "In some countries," according to Our World in Data, "it is the leading cause of death."

The city of San Francisco has a rich gay history. It is sometimes called the gay capital of the world, and historians have attributed its gay-friendly culture to its status as a frontier town and as a port city. Its first gay bar, Out, opened in 1908. In the 1960s, San Francisco was one of the first cities where openly gay candidates ran for political office. In the struggle for gay rights in the 1970s, the Castro neighborhood of San Francisco became one of the movement's headquarters, and in 1977, Harvey Milk was the first openly gay man elected to the city's board of supervisors, earning him the nickname "the mayor of Castro Street." Gay history and gay culture are inextricable from San Francisco.

Due to the city's large gay population, it was hit hard by AIDS. About 20,000 people died of AIDS in San Francisco in the 1980s. In a tight-knit community, nearly everyone knew someone who died. Many lost dozens of friends.

When we talk of AIDS memorialization, many think of the NAMES Project AIDS Memorial Quilt, with its panels of names and people who have died from the virus. The concept for the quilt was born in San Francisco in 1985, and made official by 1987. Family and friends of those who had died were desperate to memorialize their loved one, as discrimination from morgues, funeral homes, and cemeteries was common in the 1980s. Those who face discrimination in life, unfortunately, often face it in death, too. The AIDS Quilt offered mourners the opportunity to celebrate their person while acknowledging their loss in a public arena.

The AIDS Quilt still exists. At fifty-four tons, it is the largest piece of community-created art in the world, and it currently resides in San Francisco, the place where it was first imagined.

"A beautiful grove where people could find solitude and hope while remembering loved ones," the original idea for the National AIDS Memorial Grove is described in 1988, "a place to provide a positive focus for our grief." Its creators could have been describing a cemetery, though Americans' view of cemeteries, had, undoubtedly changed by the 1980s. A neglected section of Golden Gate Park, de Leveaga Dell, was selected for the location. Fundraising began in 1991, with groundbreaking done mostly by volunteers. In 1996, it was designated by Congress as a National Memorial of the United States.

Driving into the city, our plan was to visit the San Francisco Columbarium, then head over to Golden Gate Park to see the AIDS Memorial. But the columbarium was still closed to the public, due to Covid-19 restrictions. It was a foggy, overcast day. I took photographs of the gorgeous columbarium through the gate, with my son yelling that he wanted to go to the beach.

We arrived in Golden Gate Park and found the entrance to the AIDS Memorial easily. A path marked by a large boulder was surrounded by foliage. My son appropriately remarked, "a secret garden!" I reminded him that this was a sacred place and we needed to lower our voices. I noticed immediately that the boulders were a way of marking contributions to the endowment of the grove, some gifts made in memory of a specific person, others in a more general sense for the victims of AIDS by large corporations.

The path was lined with memorial benches. Stones on each side of the bench allotted space for memorial inscriptions. The first one I came across read: "We fought for love, Curtis Ingraham."

Just to the right of the entrance was a short path leading to the Circle of Friends, a long list of names arranged in a circle. The words Healing, Hope, and Remembrance mark the spot. In its center, there was a small altar made of fresh flowers. Names that jumped out to me in the circle included Harvey Milk and Elizabeth Taylor. The circle is lined with a bench allowing time for visitors to sit and meditate. On the side of the bench there was a small bowl made in the concrete, which contained several colorful paper cranes. They also hung from the nearby flowering tree.

I had lost track of my family, and so I moved farther into the grove. It was fairly quiet, and the sounds of three people playing a game of badminton were the only interruptions. The grove opened into a large lawn. My husband and son stood near another family with a small child and their Labrador, who was rolling in the grass. "Look at this DOG," my son said when he spotted me.

Continuing on the path, I noticed more memorial benches. Some were just names. Others had the most touching remembrances. "In loving memory of Taylor Phelps, Everyone's Best Friend." Another captured the atmosphere of the place: "Send in the Clowns for Steve Sem."

The grove was plainly beautiful and lush. Moisture from the fog had left a sheen on the plants. The boulders that marked contributions contributed to the natural beauty of the space. "Crossroads Circle State of California," one stated, totally benign, then devastatingly: "In memory of Women and Children lost to AIDS."

Two young women sat six feet apart on a path slightly elevated from the lawn. There were beautiful flowers near their bench, which I knew must have memorial inscriptions, but I didn't want to invade their conversation, so I gravitated toward another large rock near the stairs, labeled "Moonwalk Way," its inscription reads. "Dedicated to Douglas Watson and Larry Silva who met the day humans walked on the moon." July 20, 1969.

There was a concrete barrier of sorts and behind it a little creek with many stones. "Dry Creek," one larger one helpfully explained, "Inspired by the life of Stephen Marcus."

This beautiful unpaved path was covered by a canopy of tall trees. A couple walking their dog exited, pulling up their face masks while saying hello. All along the path there were memorial stones. "I'll love you forever and a day and a couple hours more,

Michael E. Henderson—Ande." A bouquet of wilting pink roses leaned against it.

Though this section is called Dry Creek, on that day, probably from recent storms, there was in fact water running through the creek, its babbling sound only adding to the peaceful atmosphere. At the back of the creek there is another area with benches and inscriptions where you can sit and stay a while. There were two families with kids, the adults wearing face masks and carrying on a conversation while their children picked up small rocks and threw them into the creek. I tried my best to navigate around them, maintaining a six-foot distance, while photographing the benches. At one point, I almost lost my footing.

Along the other side of the creek there was another path headed back toward the lawn. "Paul Joseph Millam, Life - Beauty - Passion." A couple walking their dog apologized for blocking my way. The trees were remarkable.

My son and I jealously eyed the pizza the other family with the dog was eating. A stone nearby read, "In memory of every Nun of the Above, Sisters of Perpetual Indulgence." Turns out, the Sisters of the Perpetual Indulgence is a group of street performers that use religious iconography (like the habits of runs) to bring awareness to religious hypocrisy and bigotry, founded in 1979, in San Francisco.

Now we were rounding our way back to the Circle of Friends. There was another large grove with a creek of stones, dotted with larger memorials throughout. "In memory of the parents we lost to AIDS, Love, The Recollectors." I was familiar with their work as I follow them on Instagram—the site is a space for children to remember the parents they lost to the virus. As you can imagine, these stories are a deeply moving and important history of loss.

A small boy about my son's age played in the stones near the front of the grove. I heard his mother call him by name, my husband's name. We all laughed at the coincidence.

"El Grupo honors Latinos and communities around the world whose lives were shortened by AIDS, Siempre Juntos, Always Together."

Another stone was inscribed with a musical quotation, notes on a staff, and the words "thank you for the dance."

It was nearing time to go, and no one wanted to leave. My son ran a few paces in front of me in this "secret garden." "It's so beautiful here," he said quietly.

A plaque on our way to our car recognized Nancy Pelosi, "who worked tirelessly on behalf of people with AIDS, was instrumental in securing national status for the Aids Memorial Grove in 1996, and has spent many hours tending this garden of serenity, renewal, and hope." I hadn't known Nancy Pelosi was involved in

the memorial grove, but it makes sense. At the time the grove was given national status, she was a congresswoman from California. There is a whole street named for her in Golden Gate Park. At the time I stood reading this plaque, she is the first woman Speaker of the House, currently fighting for Congress to pass a relief package for the current pandemic.

In addition to the commemoration of the individual lives lost, the AIDS Memorial Grove unites its memory through the experience of death. "Although we all die, we don't die in the same way," Christine Smallwood wrote about David Wojnarowicz's retrospective at the Whitney. Referencing specifically those devastating photographs the Wojnarowicz took of Hujar moments after his death from AIDS, "this particular death was not inevitable," Smallwood emphasizes. "It was bound up in the choices of a society that did not value AIDS victims enough to work harder to save them."

As I buckled my son into his car seat and fastened my own seat belt, the specter of AIDS loomed as I checked the endless news cycle for any updates on Covid-19. The adrenaline generated by being in the memorial grove, in looking and seeing, had kept me warm. Suddenly chilled, I reached over to turn on the heat.

PART II

DEATH & CO.

PORTRAITS OF
COLMA

"Wait," I said to my husband, just as we were about to drive into Greenlawn Cemetery, in Colma. There was a rather large sign. Even from the car I could clearly see the icon of a camera with a giant red X drawn through it. "Uh oh," I said, getting out to take a closer look. "Photography is not allowed in this cemetery without prior approval of the cemetery authority." We made an immediate retreat, as it wasn't clear to me whether or not the sign applied only to Greenlawn or to Greenlawn and the directly adjacent Greek Orthodox Memorial Park.

Many cemetery wanderers are budding photographers. Cemeteries make great subjects for photography. They are beautiful, curious, and absolutely still. Visiting any cemetery for the first time I always pause to make note of the rules and regulations, which are usually posted near the entrance gates. I expect to see notes about the hours—most close around 4:30 p.m., or dusk—rules on flowers or other mementos, and cultural provisions. Most are open daily, but often Jewish cemeteries are closed on Saturdays in observation of the Sabbath.

I estimate I've visited hundreds of cemeteries, and with the exception of a few indoor mausoleums, I have never encountered a sign that prohibits photography on cemetery grounds. Commercial video and photography, sure—but personal photography? Not once.

Greenlawn and the Greek Orthodox cemeteries are located in Colma, America's only necropolis. A wonder for cemetery explorers, sixteen cemeteries call this planned city of the dead home. The number was once seventeen, but that one has become a golf course. You could write an entire book about Colma and indeed, many have. If you are looking for a guidebook on Colma, look no further than Michael Svanevik and Shirley Burgett's *City of Souls*, which has been indispensable in my own research.

The cemeteries of Colma exist on many planes: as unique, individual burial grounds, as graveyards of certain ethnic or religious groups, and as active cemeteries that still serve the communities of the Bay Area. Many were founded when San Francisco evicted its cemeteries from the city. A few existed before, and a great majority accepted burials from San Francisco. Colma is its own community now, but it also stands as a record of San Francisco's failure to manage its history in the face of rapid urban development. Of the 130,000 people who were exhumed from their graves in the city, many ended up in mass graves in Colma, united under a single marker, or, in some cases no monument at all.

I have chosen portraits of Colma that I feel speak to its unique history and its relation to the Bay Area as a whole. In addition to being a safe haven for the displaced dead of the city, Colma was a place of solace for immigrant groups who faced racism and discrimination from other cemeteries and mortuaries. As much as we'd like to think we live in a post-racial society, it is crystal clear that we do not. Racism continues to affect Americans in life as it does in death. It is a disease for which there is no cure.

Graveyards are highly stigmatized places in our culture, thanks to our distant relationship with death. But in Colma, the dead outnumber the living 1,000 to 1. "Despite many millions of permanent residents, there is not a single ghostly tale or legend associated with the town," according to *City of Souls*. There is no possible way that death can be marginalized here. Colma is a city incorporated expressly for dead, where the needs of the dead come first. Death is more than a part of life in Colma, it is a way of life.

Cemeteries of Colma, in order of establishment:
Holy Cross Catholic Cemetery, 1887
Home of Peace Jewish Cemetery, 1889
Hills of Eternity Jewish Cemetery, 1889
Salem Memorial Park, 1891
Cypress Lawn Memorial Park, 1892
Olivet Memorial Park, 1896
Italian Cemetery and Mausoleum, 1899

Serbian Cemetery, 1901
Eternal Home Cemetery, 1901
Japanese Cemetery, 1901
Greenlawn Memorial Park, 1903-1904
Woodlawn Memorial Park, 1904
Sunset View Cemetery, 1907 (defunct)
Greek Orthodox Memorial Park, 1935
Pet's Rest Cemetery and Crematory, 1947
Hoy Sun Cemetery, 1988
Golden Hills Memorial Park, 1994

HOLY CROSS CATHOLIC CEMETERY

Driving to Colma was the first time I'd be traveling to a cemetery in my own car—further proof that I live in California now. We exited the freeway and made our way down a busy street. There was a line of cars waiting in a Starbucks drive-through, and a car dealership to our right. A sad, defunct Babies R Us greeted us as we rounded the top of the hill. In the distance, across El Camino Real, I could see thousands upon thousands of tombstones at the bottom of San Bruno Mountain.

Holy Cross is Colma's first cemetery, founded in 1887 before the cemeteries were evicted from San Francisco. But as we drove down El Camino Real, my heart sank. Sign after sign indicated that the cemeteries were closed to the public due to Covid-19 restrictions.

But thankfully Holy Cross was open. As we passed through the gates, the sun even came out. Holy Cross is quite large, at 300 acres. When we pulled in to park, there was only one other car parked several hundred yards away. I noticed a small tombstone with many pinwheels, flowers, and the American flag, obviously recently visited. On its back was printed the Serenity Prayer:

God grant me the serenity
to accept the things I cannot change
The courage to change the things I can
And the wisdom to know the difference

As we began our first lockdown, this epitaph felt particularly apropos.

Baseball legend Joe DiMaggio is buried at Holy Cross, and purely by chance we had parked not far from his mausoleum. As I walked over to take a few photographs, my husband and son went their own way over toward a large memorial in the center of the cemetery. I stepped back to see what appeared to be a mausoleum row. One of the family names was "Hope." I heard the

sound of laughter, and saw a group of six people walking toward my husband and son. None of them were wearing masks. But at this point, thanks to incorrect information from the government, no one knew masks were effective in stopping the spread of Covid-19. We weren't wearing masks, either.

I shouted to my husband, "Be careful." He noticed the people coming toward them, with two young kids on bikes. He picked up our son and moved out of their way. I walked over toward some other stones. The light was gorgeous.

The large monument at the center of the cemetery directly down from the chapel was a large bas-relief of the Last Supper. There was a huge tablet in the ground in front of it, the resting place of one of the archbishops of San Francisco. As I walked around the tablet to take more photos, I realized all the graves laid around it were that of priests. The inscription on the opposite side of the Last Supper read: "You are a priest forever."

By this time I was well enough away from the group of strangers. But they were still there, walking up toward DiMaggio's mausoleum. With a person as famous as DiMaggio was in life, it's not uncommon for people to visit and leave mementos. In his case,

there were baseballs, bats, Yankees hats, cards, and more. I watched in disbelief as one of the members of the group picked up one of the bats and took a few swings while his friends and kids egged him on.

I'm used to being alone in the cemetery. Of course there are occasionally other visitors, like these people, but today my husband and son were in tow. I jokingly referred to them as my research assistants as my husband chased our two-year-old around the gravestones. He stopped to take my photo. When we were first placed on lockdown and our son's day care closed, I figured this book was doomed. But now that my "research assistants" have been accompanying me, it's fascinating to see other perspectives on these places, especially a two-year-old's perspective.

Holy Cross is traditional in the sense that it is large, it was founded at the turn of the twentieth century, before the big move from San Francisco, and it is Catholic. There are many granite monuments of the sort popular in the early 1900s, with typical Catholic symbology: the IHS cross, saints, Christ himself, large plots with angels and truly remarkable memorial sculpture. One angel still stood, wings intact but missing both arms. A tomb of an Italian couple was decorated with pumpkins . . . despite the fact that it was April. One obelisk under partial shade bore a portrait of Christ suffering the crown of thorns. One of my all-time favorite cemetery monuments is the young woman clinging to the cross from the hymn "Rock of Ages, to the Cross I Cling." I snapped several photos of the version I found at Holy Cross. I was particularly taken with the ribbon in her hair, and her bare feet. "Hang in there," indeed.

The other celebrity at Holy Cross I wanted to see was Abigail Folger, coffee heiress and victim of the Manson Family. She is entombed in Holy Cross's gigantic and gorgeous mausoleum near the back of the cemetery. There was a long driveway leading up to it. An ornate gold-leaf panel of Jesus marks the entrance to the mausoleum with arms outstretched and a quote also in gold: "Looking for the Blessed Hope and the Coming of the Glory of

the Great God and Our Savior Jesus Christ." I let my husband know I was going inside. He and my son waited outside.

I made it to the center of the mausoleum, where there is an altar of sorts. Sunlight streamed through the window reflecting golden light off the marble. I was just about to turn down the hallway when a text message buzzed on my phone.

"You better come out," my husband said, "security is coming in after you." Uh-oh, maybe I wasn't supposed to go inside the

mausoleum. I walked briskly back toward the doors. There was indeed a female security guard just outside. We did a little dance, trying to abide by the six-foot rule. She tried to open the door for me, thought better of it, I approached then retreated. We both laughed at how ridiculous this was. Finally, I emerged. Before I could apologize, she said, "I almost locked you in!" I realized she was holding a large set of keys. It was 4:30 p.m. Of course, the cemetery was closing. "I'm glad your husband told me you were in there," she giggled. My first visit to Holy Cross and I was almost locked inside the mausoleum.

As we drove out of the cemetery, past the incredible office and chapel with a light-blue hearse parked outside, I saw the same guard waiting to close the entrance gates behind us. I waved at her, laughing. She smiled and waved back.

When I went back to Holy Cross several months later to find Abigail Folger, I was wearing a face mask, gloves, and carrying hand sanitizer. I walked back through the same large cathedral hallway, and took a left onto Abigail's corridor. The anniversary of the Manson Family murders had just passed two days before. Sharon Tate's rising star at the time of the murder sometimes overshadows the fact that the Manson Family members murdered six other people, including Folger. She had been staying with Tate at 10050 Cielo Drive in Los Angeles with her boyfriend, Wojchiech Frykowski, on August 9, 1969.

I scanned the crypts for Abigail's name, but I couldn't find her. I double-checked my directions. After some brief, panicked pacing, I found her. Her marble tablet was covered by a large newly placed bouquet. I stepped back to take a few photographs and to make note of the surroundings. After Abigail was murdered, her father, Peter Folger, conducted his own investigation into Manson, and threatened legal action against any publication about the private details of his daughter's life. I stepped closer to inspect the bouquet of flowers marking Abigail's crypt. They were still fresh. A rosary was tied around them, its cross dangling over the crypt beneath hers. Sticking in the middle of the bouquet was a paintbrush. Not much is known about Abigail given her father's natural inclination to protect her legacy, but she studied art history and was passionate about art. Whoever left the paintbrush in the bouquet knew this.

OLIVET MEMORIAL PARK

As I lifted my son out of his car seat, arriving at Olivet Cemetery, I was careful not to step on the small gravestones practically on top of the curb where we'd parked. "Oh," I said to my husband, "this is the baby section."

One common memento left on graves of children, it appears, here in Colma, are pinwheels. In our house back in the East Bay, the last owner, who had lived there for forty years, had pinwheels in the back garden. My son was entranced by them, and immediately made a move to pull them out of the ground at Olivet. I calmly explained that he could look at the pinwheels but could not touch them. "They aren't ours?" he asked. "They aren't ours," I repeated.

A sweet little baby in a bonnet marked the entrance to Babyland. An adorable little boy in suspenders, just three, smiled from his small stone. Children's graves are different for me now, as a parent. I always take time to pay my respects but now I am more eager to move on from these sections.

In the distance, I could see there was a large monument between two flag poles. I made my way over to the Showfolks of America memorial. Beware, reader, if you are afraid of clowns. Erected in 1945, this memorial marks the resting of place of clowns and other vaudevillians, as the inscription reads, "that they may rest in peace among their own." A terrifying smiling clown laughs at you from the top of the monument, his disembodied head floating in front of a cityscape, with a circus tent, Ferris wheel, and other carnival rides in a primary-color tableau. A tiny cherub perches over the lip of the tomb, his hands folded shyly over his lap.

I'm not afraid of clowns, but I can see why people are. The President of the Showfolks Association's plaque lays at the front of the memorial. Earl J. Leonard, 1908–1982, "Swacko," presumably his clown name. "What that name," my son said, pointing to the clown. "That's a clown," my husband answered.

Another gigantic monument in the shape of a large bell appeared within a circle of bushes. As we got closer, I realized it

was a sculpture of a sailor at the helm of a ship. Erected March 17, 1946, it honors "mariners who died during WWII"—"and the sea shall give up its dead—from every latitude here rest our brothers of the Sailors' Union of the Pacific."

My son was thrilled with the size and scope of this monument, and we went a few rounds of hide-and-seek around its base. One of the plaques near the monument was for a man who died in 1988, a bundle of four dried sunflowers laid on top, as if they'd been left there years and years ago, untouched.

On a knoll down the hill, there were a series of tombstones with portraits, each one as incredible as the last. I've seen many

enameled portraits in Jewish cemeteries back on the East Coast, and they are also common in Catholic cemeteries. Modern technology has led to a resurgence in photo portraits and etched portraits in granite. These, though, at Olivet, were the first Asian portraits I've seen from the 1920s to the 1960s.

The "Look" family, with Ma, Pa, and little Mary, who died at nine years old, were my introduction to these sort of graves, which have become a precious record to a vibrant Asian community in San Francisco in the mid-century and beyond. A young woman, "beloved mother," with only the date of death, Feb. 11, 1952, sporting wire-framed glasses and pin curls, smiled shyly back from her tombstone. Finally, the Owyang family, another Asian family, Fred, Rose, and little Terry, just four. I took several photos of this stone before a chill came over me. They all had the same date of death, 1952. I looked at their smiling faces. Illness. I told myself, it was illness.

I posted the image of their tombstone in hopes that someone would know more about their fates. A genealogist responded:

"I was able to locate a newspaper article in The Bradford Era from Bradford, Pennsylvania dated February 18, 1952," she said. "It states that Rose, Fred, Terry, and Rose's sister May and Rose and May's mother were shot by May's estranged husband Donald Lum . . . and then he shot himself. So sad."

When you read the uniform death dates on a family stone in a cemetery, you hope for illness. Your brain goes next to an accident: a car crash. This sort of violence is devastating. Murder. When I first posted the photo, several people wrote in, eager to know the story. Portraits on gravestones emphasize the fact that every one

of these markers contains a person, a life, and a personality. The enormous loss in this one single family.

Tombstones and records can just become names and dates. The Owyangs' story, in its violence and tragedy, made them modern in my mind. Like the young woman beside them, with her sly look and glasses, they could be my contemporaries, my friends.

The light that day was spectacular. A bright, sunny day with few clouds. Toward the main drive, I noticed an unusual monument—at first it looked like a typical in-ground crypt cover, a concrete slab. As I got closer I realized it was a bed, with two tasseled pillows labeled Father and Mother.

A stately obelisk revealed some fantastic names: America Moore, born in Kentucky. Her sister, or sister-in-law, Maria Bacon. I wondered how the family came to live in the Bay Area. Atop a weathered plaque nearby rested a blue-and-white ceramic jug filled with rainwater.

Just across the path a gorgeous mausoleum in the Greco-Roman style wreathed with carved leaves begged for gawking.

The stunning bronze door featured a barred round window with a weeping lily and its lower half a recently extinguished torch, still smoking, festooned with a bow and laurel. Inside, the family vault in white granite contained two beautiful marble urns and the crypts of the Beckers, including Bernhard A. Becker, "pioneer of 1849."

A large slab crypt across the way bore a lengthy epitaph but got right to the point in the end: "He lived and died an honest man."

The landscapers were out, with their Weedwackers and leaf blowers. We strolled up the path, trying to stay out of their way. "I don't think I will ever get used to the palm trees," I said to my husband. One section on the hill was simply perfect in the morning sunlight, all the tombstones with the open-book design on top, the Book of Life. It looked like a small outdoor library, where everyone reading had simply gotten up for lunch, leaving the pages open, eerily still.

As we crossed back to the car, my husband grabbed my arm. "What is that?" he said, pointing just over a section. In broad daylight in a cemetery, this can be a disconcerting question. I looked over quickly, also gauging where my son was, and asking him sternly to come closer. It was a dog—no, a fox—bounding through the tombstones. Too large to be a fox. "It's a coyote," I said. "Come here," I repeated to my son, picking him up.

Two landscapers on a little truck appeared. We weren't wearing masks, and neither were they—it's disturbing to think that at this point the government had told us masks were useless. But we

kept our distance, standing about fifteen feet away. "What was that?" my husband asked them. "It's a dog," one man said, indicating there was a language barrier and making me regret that I had taken French in high school. "A coyote?" I asked. He nodded. "He lives here," he said. "He's always been here."

We thanked them as they drove on. I kept my eye on the coyote, the only thing bouncing between the many tombstones.

ITALIAN CEMETERY

As you enter the main drive of the Italian Cemetery in Colma, the uniformity of color is what strikes you first—the chrome of the granite reflecting off the white marble in the hot sun makes the family crypts look like shiny metal. Rows upon rows of elevated tombs with the cross, portraits, icons of the Virgin greet you like gleaming new cars at a dealership. At the end of the long road of graves a creamy yellow chapel dotted with green stands in the distance.

When we arrived at the Italian Cemetery, the sun was shining, though the fog still stood at the base of Mount Bruno. The Italian names and faces beam back from their stones, gleaming with pride. I went to Italy on my honeymoon. After that trip I understood the pride Italians have for their home. It is simply one of the most beautiful places in the world, not to mention the warmth and culture of their cuisine, religion, and disposition.

This same pride is reflected in the glare from these stones. The color palette looks like something out of the sea. The lighter color of granite, all hues of light gray, blending against the blue sky. There is only one section of lawn, a bright pop of green in an otherwise sea of white, blue, and gray.

Italians were one of the first groups to immigrate widely to the United States. Their presence and influence is well-known in New York, but they also made their mark on the West Coast. By the time the Italian Cemetery was founded in 1899, Holy Cross, Colma's Catholic Cemetery, had already been open for twelve years. Though the archbishop felt there wasn't a need for another Catholic cemetery in Colma and refused to consecrate this ground, the demand for an Italian cemetery on top of an already existing Catholic one indicates the large Italian population in the Bay Area at this time.

During the 1918–1919 flu epidemic in which 500,000 Americans died, "five sections of Holy Cross were filled," and one complete section of the Italian Cemetery, according to Svanevik and Burgett's *City of Souls*. "In SF and along the peninsula, health officials reported that the epidemic struck with greatest savagery in Chinatown and predominately Italian North Beach (districts of San Francisco) and both Colma and South San Francisco where the immigrant population was greatest."

Immigrant families generally live in close proximity to each other, frequently in the same residence, as is the Italian practice. Traditionally, adult children do not leave the family home until they are married. During a pandemic, the risk of transmission among immigrant families and communities is particularly high.

The devastating effect of the flu epidemic is easy to see in these tombstones by death dates, particularly in those of the young. While we think of the elderly being at high risk of death from disease, with certain viral illnesses the immune response of younger people, what's known as a "cytokine storm" when the body releases too many proteins to fight off infection too quickly, can result in death. This could be the case with Covid-19, too, though research is still ongoing.

On the other side of the ground crypts there is a line of family mausolea with gorgeous stained-glass windows in the back.

Though some of these have not been accessed since the mid-1900s, they are frozen in time, with fake flowers, religious icons, and portraits, a makeshift altar. Others reveal the inevitable passage of time with unfortunate crumbling walls and broken glass.

The incredible monuments at the Italian Cemetery, and in all of the cemeteries in Colma, in fact, all over the Bay Area come from monument makers based in Colma, like Bocci Memorials, founded in 1896, and V. Fontana & Co., founded in 1921. Both of these families are Italian, and both companies are family-owned and -operated.

A stunning angel greets me as I make my way down the path, her arm raised with one finger pointing to the heavens. There is a beautiful portrait of what appears to be a young bride, Maria, wearing a white dress and veil. "Rest in peace, cara figlia." She died at fourteen—let's hope her white veil was for her first communion, not her wedding. This memorial sculpture is a complete work of art, and in excellent shape considering the fact that Maria died in 1903. Set against her portrait are engraved leaves of ivy, symbolizing immortality through its evergreen nature, with a rosebud

garland, indicating the loss of a young woman, and a star on the pedestal that the angel stands upon.

I had just about made my way to the church at the end of the row when I noticed a large mausoleum to my right. The doors were open. I pulled up my face mask, and, to be honest, held my breath. There was an incredible pink light filtering through a gigantic stained-glass window of roses and lilies, brilliant pink, green, and white, giving the entire crypt a rosy glow. This is the cemetery's

oldest structure, what was once the receiving vault, built in 1900. While the exterior concrete has undergone some wear and tear, the interior Carrara marble is nearly pristine. The gorgeous window, the original destroyed by earthquake, is a restoration that was completed in 1992.

An angel stands by the doorway holding an offering basket in the shape of a shell. Under the "Receiving Vault Directory" sign is a helpful list of its occupants with their locations.

On my way back out to the main path, another angel, deep in thought, holding a flower crown, caught my eye. "In memory of mother and father," her pedestal read, and in place of a traditional portrait, there was a photo of a black-veiled woman kneeling at a small table lit with candles. The inscription at the bottom of the image reads, "praying for my beloved mother."

Just next door, a family monument of brothers and sisters, two incredibly young brothers close enough in age to look like twins, eyed me cynically, dressed in matching black suits with gigantic white bows.

I did a double-take passing a family mausoleum with the name: I. FAUCI. Dr. Fauci? I wondered aloud.

I had reached the baby section. The tombstones occupy the only part of the cemetery on green lawn. Their single tombstones are smaller but still topped with icons of the Saints, the Virgin, a lamb, or Christ himself. They stand in a perfect line like some horrible chessboard.

An infant's photo, swaddled in a blanket, just opening his eyes to the world, who lived just over two months. A sweet baby girl on a bearskin rug who died just before her first birthday. A gorgeous marble stone for a young man, just three, who stands defiantly before the camera, buried here in 1927. A stone with a heart-wrenching typographical error, our "beloving" rather than "beloved." Parents who lost a child at just four months old, and then horribly, his brother, at three. An adorable little girl, smiling and clutching her doll. There are too many to name, and yet, you want to name them all.

One particularly ornate gravestone featured a little boy's portrait and was decorated with a cowboy's hat and holster, an unoccupied bicycle on top. "Baby Santo," Sainted baby, holy baby. Later research revealed he had drowned in a San Francisco reservoir, six years old. His friend tried to grab his shirt, "but could not hold on."

Walking through the family crypts, some held as many as nine or ten people, their portraits a family album. A wind blew in, blowing my hair in my face as I wished I'd brought something to tie it back. Just like that, the sunshine was gone. An ominous reminder: "Una morta ci disguinse . . . un'altra ci congiunge." "One death separates us, another connects us."

Italian blood and the identification with the culture is strong in the United States, even in California, where there is a greater influx of Asian immigrants due to simple geography. I am only one-fourth Italian, probably—though I carry my father's name, Ferri, which means "iron." An Italian teacher I had in college told me it was a very common name in Italy, probably meaning my ancestors were blacksmiths—like the name "Smith" in English.

A handsome young man who died at just twenty-six smiles back from his tombstone. Born in Mexico, his epitaph is in Spanish: "Su inconsolable madre decider este recuerado a su memoria." "His inconsolable mother dedicates this memorial to his memory."

Just next to him, a plain wooden cross for Teresa, who died, unbelievably, in 1910.

The Italian Cemetery is filled with young brides and portraits of first communions, whose stoic faces stare back from their memorial portraits. Manuelina was born in Riva Tricozo, Italy, and died in San Francisco in 1910, at the age of 22. She looks friendly, a white pouf hat balancing precariously on her head, but unsure. A fifteen-year-old girl, gorgeous in her white dress and veil, stares unsmiling into the camera. Another bride, just down the path, whose epitaph is barely legible, looks directly at the camera with blazing light eyes.

Another set of brothers stand awkwardly side by side in their dual portrait. Their tombstone is topped by a gorgeous and unusual statue of a little girl holding flowers in her dress, a cross draped around her neck. Her little chubby legs and baby feet are shockingly lifelike.

A young boy, just ten years old, stares confidently from his tombstone. His epitaph reads: "Rapito inesorabilmente all'affezione dei genitori," "kidnapped inexorably from his parents' affection" in 1915.

An absolutely stunning family plot, belonging to the family Calegari, features a marble bust of a smiling woman wreathed with roses, and a dashing mustachioed man on top of its obelisk, with a floppy hat. The memorial was built by the husband for his wife who was "kidnapped in the prime of life by accidental misfortune . . . she was a virtuous woman and much adored." He signs off on his monument by telling her to "enjoy eternal peace beloved bride."

A flair for poetry must run in the family. Just underneath their ancestors are more Calegaris who died in 2007, 2008, 2009, and 2015, including another husband and wife. Husband followed wife in death four years later, his "heart held her love until they shared it in the eternal life."

A stunning obelisk features an anchor, a common Christian symbol, but upon further inspection, I recognized it as an anchor cross thanks to Douglas Keister's excellent *Stories in Stone*, a book on cemetery symbols and iconography. A cross in disguise, common in "coastal cities," its appearance as an anchor allowed Christians to proclaim their faith in secrecy. This one was particularly beautiful, interlaid with a bouquet and a winged staff.

By this time, the sun had completely disappeared and the weather had turned ominous. Windblown, my husband and son had returned to the car. I ran down mausoleum row, trying to see as much as possible. An incredible statue of the Archangel Michael stood atop a family tomb, pointing daintily up to the sky with one figure, his taut torso covered in scaled armor and his feet clad in beautiful gladiator sandals.

One stone caught my eye for its tasseled pillow, "in memory of my dear husband," and just below, there is a small bear. A bear can be a Christian symbol, but given the location, in Colma, and the fact that this man was a "member of San Francisco Parlor,"

I wonder if the bear is a nod to the California Republic flag, designed by a group of American settlers who tried to break away from Mexico in 1846, chosen as a symbol of stubborn power. Though the symbol has endured, civilization had other plans for the California grizzly bear. By the Gold Rush era, most of the grizzlies were captured and killed. Now extinct, the last California grizzly was spotted in Sequoia State Park in 1924, walking away, never to be seen again.

WOODLAWN MEMORIAL PARK

Three Asian cherubs, carved in marble, greeted us at Woodlawn, hanging over the stone of a young boy like good friends. "May your adventures in heaven and the infinite keep you happy and busy until we meet again. Love forever, Mommy, Daddy, Michael, and Matthew." There was a portrait of the boy, who had died at just fifteen. The cherubs were all in his likeness. Then I realized they weren't all angels. Only one had wings. The other two were his surviving brothers.

Woodlawn Cemetery in Colma was established in 1904, just after burials were prohibited in San Francisco. There are plenty of memorials of that time here, on a hill behind its castle looking main building, which contains a chapel and a crematorium. But there are also many contemporary, traditional Chinese monuments, with their uniform design on the front hill, closest to a more modern crypt. Woodlawn prides itself on its understanding and offering of Chinese funeral and burial customs. On the day we visited, the cemetery was busy. There were several families coming to pay their respects to loved ones, nearly all of them in this front Chinese section.

One epic family tomb featured a modern engraving of the Golden Gate Bridge. Just behind it, up the hill, were sections of traditional Victorian mourning statuary, most of them erected just a year or two after the cemetery's founding in Colma. There were also monuments clearly older than the cemetery itself, including one rock of ages for a Melville Cox who died in 1869, aged fourteen years. These are the graves that were moved from San Francisco.

What had begun as a foggy, chilly day had developed into full sun with blue skies. I peeled off my jacket. A gorgeous bronze monument of a large urn protected by two laureled ladies looked

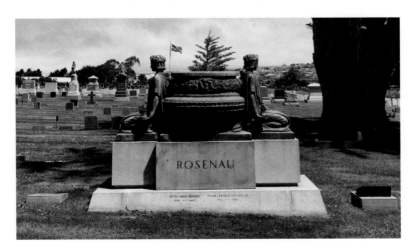

perfect set against the still hanging fog in the background. My son picked dandelions nearby, and the sprinklers in a section across from us turned on. The grounds, with their bright green lawn, were impeccably kept.

Completely by accident, we had found John Daly, the man for whom Daly City is named, a California businessman who opened the city's first bank. Originally from Boston, Daly had traveled to California with his mother, who caught yellow fever on the journey and died. He traveled on to San Francisco alone, at just thirteen years old. Working in the dairies allowed him to save up enough money to buy a significant amount of land in San Mateo. After the 1906 earthquake, he sold lots of the land to many in need of a new home. He died in 1923 at the age of eighty-one. At the time of his death he was married to a woman named Florence Smart, but here at Woodlawn, there appears to have been a wife who predeceased him, Lillie Frances, who died in 1912.

On the other side of the path there was a newer tombstone, its engraving of a rose caught my eye. The woman buried here also bore the name "Daly," and I wondered if she were a relative. "The

roses in our rose garden will bloom forever," her epitaph read.

A spectacular obelisk with a circular bronze portrait of the bearded deceased, surrounded by carved mourning drapery and the Freemason symbol was difficult to ignore. "For many years and at his death, an officer of the United States's Mint." At the bottom of his monument, his "Angel Mother . . . Gone but not forgotten." These monuments were all moved from the city. Another, for a man who died in 1875. "The sun is set while tis yet day."

A young woman smiled from her beautiful tombstone, carved with daffodils. "In memory of my inspiration, a devoted wife and loving mother."

The stones down the path were a jumble of eras—German immigrants, Italians, Chinese families, Victorian-era urns and more modern tombstones, side by side. One stone, with clearly Chinese names but a German epitaph: "With the Lord in Ewigkeit Amen." For eternity, amen. The sprinkler system came on as we dashed to safety. One granite portrait with the epitaph: "A legend of San Francisco, co-founder of 'Foxy Lady Boutique,' Singer, Actor, Entertainer, Loved by All." For the first time ever, I saw

Palestinian graves, a small section, all bearing the Palestinian flag. "Surely we belong to Allah and to Him we shall return."

One beautiful stone with a heart design laureled with flowers caught my eye. There was a portrait of a young woman named Francesca Carole in what looked like a graduation photo. "Always in our hearts," she had died at just eighteen in 1970. Research revealed this young woman was killed along with several of her friends in a horrible car crash near the Golden Gate Bridge.

Francesca and her friends were piled into a Mustang when a Porsche coming off the bridge slammed into their car at nearly 100 miles per hour. Nine people were killed, the highest death toll in a traffic accident in San Francisco at the time. The accident made national news, and was even reported by the *New York Times*. When I posted a photo of Francesca's stone on my Instagram, several people commented that they remembered the crash.

As I read through the original news reports on my phone, I realized that I was standing here, at her grave, exactly fifty years from the date of the accident, an insane coincidence. What had caught my eye was Francesca's heart, and her portrait. Or was it something else?

By now we had reached the front section of Woodlawn, with mostly Chinese graves, and it was busy. As I stopped to photograph a large sculpture of Psalm 121 at the front of the mausoleum, several cars pulled up with mourners, all sporting face masks. A young man prayed in the distance in front of one stone, openly weeping and raising his arms to the heavens. We made swift moves to get back to the car.

After I strapped my son into his car seat, though, I noticed some unusual sculptures in the adjoining section. I told my husband I needed to see it before we left, and ran over. In front of a large in-ground family tomb, obviously Chinese, stood four ladies—in sculpted in white marble, their dresses marbleized red and white. They appeared to be holding something, fruit of some kind, one held a bundle of grapes, another a bouquet of roses. They reminded me of the Three Graces. They are China's "four beauties." Though some of them were real women, others exhibit more mythological qualities, Xi Shi, Wang Zhaojun, Diaochan, and Yang Guifei, who all lived in different dynasties. The power of their beauty was such that generals and entire kingdoms fell under their spell—even a flock of geese were momentarily distracted, forgot to flap their wings, and crashed to the ground.

As we searched for the exit I realized I had missed a major monument I wanted to see, statues of Snow White and the Seven Dwarves that protect the "Children's Sanctuary" section of the cemetery. We drove around several times, eyes peeled, searching for the little statues. Nothing. We had a hungry toddler in the back seat, and my husband was losing his patience.

I got out of the car and figured I'd walk where the section was supposed to be and eventually I'd find it. I was in the right

place—there were children's graves. One had an offering of flowers and clementines that looked like they'd just been left there. Another's epitaph: "Sweet William . . . Forever our little boy." I looked back at the horizon, and noticed a plaque. Children's Sanctuary! This was it.

"And He said:
Suffer the little children
To come unto me,
For such is the
Kingdom of Heaven."

But where were Snow White and her seven dwarves?

I looked down. There was a sizable tablet in the ground made of gravel, and eight little spots untouched by sun, obviously where the statues had once stood. No wonder I couldn't spot them from the road: they weren't there. In Tom Jokinen's 2010 book, *Curtains: Adventures of an Undertaker in Training*, he learned that the statues had been smashed by vandals. "Woodlawn wanted to rebuild the sculpture, but Disney preferred they didn't," he reports a manager explaining. "I believe it had something to do with money."

When Jokinen was there, there was part of Dopey still standing, as if he'd been blown up by a landmine. Now all that remains are empty eight spots.

SERBIAN CEMETERY

"Watch your step," I called out to my husband, in the midst of applying sunscreen to our son. The ground at the Serbian Cemetery was patchy, powdery red dirt. Step in the wrong place and your whole foot sinks into the ground. It was a hot day—as usual, I was overdressed.

"Serbian" is a misnomer. Not all the people buried here are Serbian, but they are all Orthodox Christians: Serbian, Russian, Ukrainian, Greek, Armenian, and more. Most of the stones bear

the Orthodox cross, with a slanted line drawn down the middle, or a straight extra horizontal line under the first. They are mostly marble, in-ground plots, with epitaphs written in Cyrillic or English. Almost all feature a red and gold eternal flame candle. The uniformity is such the cemetery resembles a military burial ground.

In most sections there is barely an inch or two between the slabs. In others, there are large patches of dirt, and some graves without a marble marker, only a wooden handmade cross. At first I thought these might be new graves, but they were decades old. Most of the older graves feature enameled photograph portraits of the deceased. Due to the sameness of much of the tombstone design, those who break the mold stand out: one had a beautiful engraving of a sunflower growing up the side of the granite.

One particularly impressive Cadillac-sized black marble grave stopped me in my tracks. A smiling engraved portrait of a beautiful young woman smiled back at me. A quick search revealed that she had been killed in a gas explosion in 2019. Her tomb includes a lengthy epitaph from her family and a caduceus, as she had been in medical school at the time of her death. There was a fresh bouquet of carnations and a slightly wilting bouquet of roses at the foot of her grave, the sign of a recent visit. But today, we were totally alone—there were no other people in the cemetery.

The Serbian Cemetery was founded in 1901 when burials had been prohibited inside the city limits—the reason why many of Colma's cemeteries were founded this year. The cemetery is not large, and the land is nearly completely flat. Behind the cemetery, a tractor on a small flower farm buzzed away, and directly in front, facing Hillside Boulevard, is the pet cemetery, Pet's Rest. A lower level with a gorgeous chapel and the official entrance gates buffer the section directly next to the street.

While my family walked over to a large monument in the center of the cemetery, I made my way to a standing wall crypt near the back. There was a gigantic tractor trailer parked back here, and a clanking sound from within. I thought maybe there was someone

at work, but as I got closer I saw it was just a swinging clamp at the back of the truck, as if someone had just closed it and walked away.

The wall crypt at the back of the cemetery is built in a V with an island in the cemetery for niches. The concrete material has weathered over the years, but the gold mosaic at the center sparkled in the sunlight. There were several bouquets left in the wall vases, mostly fake flowers, and eternal flame candles. A plaque

reads: "This mausoleum dedicated to our Russian brothers in faith, First Serbian Benevolent Society, May 8, 1976."

The portraits of the residents of the Serbian Cemetery reveal distinguished people, formal, elegant, even glamorous. One couple had their passions in life ringed around their portraits: for her, a lute, for him, a painter's palette and brush. Another couple had a sculpted rendition of the cathedral in Red Square emerging from the side of their tombstone.

I can read a little French, Italian, and German, but the Cyrillic alphabet really throws a wrench in the works, particularly for names, which are not so easily translated. One translation app came through with "uppa Heaven!" A few more attempts revealed, "arms of Heaven!"

A marble cross emerging from a rock with a small angel at prayer festooned with gorgeous roses bore a large color portrait of a young woman, "beloved wife and mother," who died young at just twenty-seven. "That's a pretty lady," my son said. "Mama," I said. "Mama," he repeated, "like my Mama."

Across the narrow paved road there were more and more plots. One stood out for its beautiful cherry blossom design, in bright pink, it popped against the plain dark and light gray of the other granite tombstones. I posted this photo on my Instagram. A follower commented that the name was Armenian—and that judging from the dates on the tombstones the family may have fled the Armenian genocide between 1914 and 1923.

Many of the community cemeteries in Colma, cemeteries organized by religion, ethnicity, or country, are the result of major waves of immigration to California, to the Bay Area after wartime, genocide, economic depression, and revolution. The Russian Revolution, from 1917 to 1923, drove many to seek a new life in the United States. Once these families had arrived and settled in San Francisco they built tight-knit communities in the city, but were met with discrimination when it came to religious beliefs and burial practices. As cemeteries were being met with more regulations in San Francisco, Colma presented itself not only as a option for burial, but as a burial place that reflected their community.

I had wondered the entire time about a large, metal sculpture of some kind at the center of the cemetery. Upon closer inspection it appeared to be dedicated to the "Honorary Members of the First Serbian Benevolent Society." The first three members were princes and and kings. This gigantic piece of metal looked awfully strange in the center of a cemetery. It looked like a piece of a spacecraft . . . like Sputnik.

My camera functions as my notepad in the cemetery. Often my time is limited, and I'll snap a photo instead of writing something down because I always refer back to my pictures, especially if there's something mysterious that warrants further research. Such was the case with one grave on my way to the little church at the front of the cemetery.

There was a beautiful cross with a portrait of an elderly woman with a Russian name who had died in 1967. But in her plot, there were two granite slabs in the ground. One with a portrait "beloved mother" who had died in 1999. Then there was a plaque with no dates, just names and portraits of two siblings. They looked so young, in their late teens.

I did a search for their names. These two teenagers, brother and sister, had hitchhiked from Las Vegas when their friend's car broke down in 1978. They never made it back to their home of Barstow, California. Nearly a month later their bodies were discovered by a sheepherder. Jacqueline was 18, her brother Malcolm 17.

For twenty-five years the case went cold. The man who killed Jacqueline and Malcolm was a braggart and gossiped about his crimes in jail, eventually leading to him producing evidence, a turquoise ring that had belonged to Jacqueline, that tied him to the case. Though a trial was supposed to be forthcoming as of 2004, I couldn't find any information over whether or not it had actually come to pass. He was convicted of a different murder in 1973. As a serial killer, he won't be leaving jail.

I walked down a small set of stairs directly behind the church. Embedded into the wall there were small niches for cremains. One beautiful young woman's portrait marked by an artificial purple pansy seemed to have an inner glow. I rounded the corner and found several tombs of Russian Orthodox priests, featuring incredible portraits in their traditional hats, long beards, robes and crucifixes. These graves occupy a place of deep importance and respect judging from their proximity to the church. On the flagpoles in front, Russian, American, and California flags whipped wildly in the breeze. But to my disappointment, the church was closed due to Covid-19 restrictions. I sighed in frustration as I pressed up against the glass, shielding my eyes from the powerful sun.

The stained glass above the entrance to the church featured an all-knowing eye, lest I pull any fast moves. The interior was stunning. The back panel behind an altar presented the Virgin with arms outstretched and two smaller panels, one of the Virgin holding the Christ child, the Annunciation scene between them in beautiful light blue, and a portrait of the adult Christ in the midst of a blessing. A section to the right of the altar depicts the resurrection of Christ. The carpet was crimson and recently vacuumed.

A young soldier in his cap smiled reassuringly from his memorial portrait. He had died in action in Duren, Germany, during World War II. He had been just twenty years old.

My son ran up the ramp to see the brilliant gold mosaic panel in a two-floor wall crypt at the cemetery's northern border. "Who's that," he asked. "Jesus Christ," I said. "Jesus Christ," he repeated softly.

We had entered a Greek section. An occasional flowering bush accompanied the graves, which listed birthdates. "Born in Errikousa, Corfu, Greece." The mausoleum had fresh flowers in place, and "Big Joe," a forklift for caskets. I was running out of time. My husband and son made it back to the air-conditioned car while I scanned the front rows of the cemetery and the original entrance gates. Nearly every stone was worth looking at. My eyes were tired.

One family had lost two children, one at five in 1931 and her brother, just two, in 1940. Another epitaph included a note from

the deceased's children and grandchildren: "Dear Lord, please receive our beloved mom and dad in thy kingdom for their great love, kindness, and compassion to mankind."

Across the path I found a Baroness Jadwiga Lewis of Menar and daughter Anna. Menar is in Northwest India. Just a few steps away I found an entire family, grandparents, mother, and son with portraits. The son was awfully young and handsome. He had died in 1959 at the age of fourteen.

Gorgeous couples smiled from wedding photos and individual portraits. Another man's epitaph proudly stated, "Chemical Engineer." Epic mustaches from the turn of the twentieth century confirmed the glamour of the Serbian Cemetery's occupants. At this point, my family was ready to go. I ran up and down the wall crypt, snapping photos as quickly as I could. It was hot. I looked down at my sunburned forearms, and we went home.

Later that week, I returned to the portrait of the handsome teenager. A newspaper search revealed that he had been electrocuted by kite. "14-year-old . . . electrocuted when his kite struck a high tension line at the rear of his home."

CHINESE CEMETERIES

Just across the street from the back gate of Cypress Lawn are the two Chinese cemeteries of Colma: Hoy Sun and Golden Hill. On another unseasonably hot day, I walked into Golden Hill. There was one family making an offering to their loved one, chatting loudly and laughing at the tombstone. All were wearing face masks and sun hats.

I looked back at the cemetery itself: the stones were completely uniform, mostly all the same maroon granite, some dark gray or light gray, their names and epitaphs the only differentiation.

There is a slight hill up toward the foot of the mountain, but Golden Hill is mostly flat. Feng shui is incredibly important in Chinese burial traditions. A good view is essential to a good afterlife. If a grave is located in a poor location, it is said to bring misfortune on the entire surviving family. Not wanting to disturb the group at the front of the cemetery, I crossed the path and made my way to the back.

Some of the tombstones were adorned with lotus symbols and fortune tassels and bore photo portraits of the deceased. In Chinese tradition, according to *City of Souls*, tombstones for spouses are made at the same time. The name of the deceased is painted in white and the name of the living spouse in red. At their time of death, it is painted over in white by the monument maker.

Near the back of the cemetery there was a large John Deere excavator, completely still and unoccupied, parked on the side of the drive. This is not an unusual appearance in a cemetery. But when I rounded the corner I noticed there was a gold crypt sitting just underneath the claw of the tractor, ready for interment.

Golden Hill was founded in 1994. Chinese cemeteries are new to Colma, as for many years in the Bay Area, and the United States as a whole, the practice was for benevolent societies to disinter burials and send bones back to China to be buried with their ancestors. When the People's Republic of China took control in 1949, this

practice became extremely challenging. Combined with the fact that many Chinese immigrants began to see America as their home, more and more chose to be buried permanently in California.

I walked up the hill and over a small rock wall, not realizing I had just entered the next cemetery, Hoy Sun. There was a large pine tree with shade where I had hoped to take a break, but as soon as I passed into this cemetery, I noticed a family approaching with their container for offerings, so I made haste to the front.

As in Golden Hill, nearly all of the tombstones in Hoy Sun are completely uniform, the same color, the same design, obviously created by the same monument maker. The graves in this section were recent, most from the late 1990s and early 2000s. Hoy Sun is a bit older than Golden Hill, founded in 1988. While all Colma cemeteries are open to Chinese burials, and some like Wood-lawn offer specialization in Chinese ritual, many families choose these specifically demarcated burial grounds. As more and more

Chinese families began to choose to stay in the United States for burial, nonsectarian cemeteries ran out of space, necessitating the need for specifically Chinese cemeteries.

On the hill of Hoy Sun, there was a metal offering can still smoking as I passed by. Families burn paper money at the grave so that the deceased will have the funds to buy whatever they need in the next world. Its also common to see water and fruit, usually oranges, left at the gravesite.

As I made my way down the hill to the Hoy Sun office building, a young couple was preparing to make their offering. Carrying a jug of water, the man smiled and said "hello." The grounds staff sat in a small shed off to my right, taking shelter from the heat. "Hi," I said, as they watched me, a lone white woman in a Chinese cemetery, walk past. "Oh, hi," one replied, confused.

According to *City of Souls*, two foo dogs, or lion dogs, guard the entrance to Hoy Sun. Protective guardians, usually one is male (with a ball) and one is female (with a cub), representing the yin and yang energy. Perhaps the two guarding the entrance to Hoy Sun were both male, because they both held a ball underfoot. I turned outside the gate to take some photographs.

On Hillside Avenue, between Golden Hill and Pet's Rest there was another cemetery. This was Sunset View, a burial ground for "paupers," established in Colma in 1907, but it was "developed" to make way for a golf course. As I walked by its location on my way to Pet's Rest, I saw the sign: "Cypress Golf Driving Range and Learning Center." According to *City of Souls*,

"remains from Sunset View have never been disinterred," meaning that any markers or stones were simply removed and the golf course was built on top. The bodies remain.

As an article from KQED points out, the fate of Sunset View is in direct opposition to the entire point of Colma's existence. "Ensuring that your final resting place is really your final resting place was the very idea behind establishing Colma as a modern-day necropolis. Yet even in Colma, the sanctity of the grave is not what it used to be. The needs and whims of the living have encroached over the years. For example, Sunset View Cemetery, a burial ground for paupers, in 1951 became a golf course."

The sign looked vintage, dating maybe from the 1980s, discolored by time. A large black Hummer came around the driveway to exit and very nearly mowed me down. The man inside raised his arm at me in anger, and yelled "what the hell?" indicating he blamed me for the near collision. In fairness, I suppose there aren't many pedestrians taking photos of the Cypress Golf Driving Range sign. I considered yelling something uncouth back at him, but thought better of it, wondering if he knew he was playing golf on top of a cemetery.

PET'S REST

Pet cemeteries allow us to grieve in an open way. Because the deceased are animals, our pets, the loss feels less serious. But pet cemeteries are more than just an outlet for sentimentality, they are a place of real loss, and most of all, they are proof of a place's culture and its families.

Pet's Rest was established in 1947 by Earl and Julia Taylor. Julia served as the office manager for Cypress Lawn. The community of people who lived and worked in Colma, like Julia and Earl, needed a place to bury their pets. Serving the Bay Area as a whole, Pet's Rest is also a crematory and offers witnessed cremation, equine cremation, and a wide range of memorial stones and urns.

Pet's Rest is listed in many a San Francisco or Bay Area guidebook as a point of interest whereas human cemeteries are not.

Pet cemeteries may be a curiosity, a tourist attraction, but on the day when we visited Pet's Rest, there were several grieving families at the office, one picking up the cremains of their beloved cat, another picking out a tombstone design for their dog. Despite the fact that Pet's Rest is just off Hillside Boulevard, it is a really lovely spot. Most of the graves are underneath a gigantic tree, in green grass with dappled sunlight. A beautiful mural adorns the side of the office building and crematory.

At a pet cemetery, there is the touching feeling of loss and a reminder of our own pets, but the overall mood is certainly friendlier. No one is suspicious of your visit or your desire to remark on the epitaphs or take photographs. In my visits to pet cemeteries I find myself wishing this attitude was more often found in human cemeteries. They are still places of remembrance. This kind of memory, in my opinion, should be encouraged. Pets are people, but people are people, too.

The first face to greet me at Pet's Rest was that of Grisha, a beautiful black pug, her sweet portrait engraved on her tombstone, "too dearly loved to be forgotten."

Plain wood markers in the shape of a fish marked the resting place of beloved goldfish, certainly a more dignified send-off than most receive.

A family plot underneath the tree had pets buried there since 1967 and as recently as 2017.

My son was thrilled with the pet cemetery, though somewhat confused. He loved all the photos and engraved portraits of the many cats and dogs, and recognized shapes of fish and sculptures of bunny rabbits, but he wanted to know where they were. We have our own dog at home, and this is not a conversation I am ready to have.

During Covid-19 our pets have become even greater support, especially for those who live alone. For families navigating Covid, pets can provide not only companionship but a chance for children to socialize and to learn essential caregiving skills while isolated from their friends and teachers.

Rusty: He was a good wolf

Good Lookin' and Checkers

The grounds of Pet's Rest are a bit treacherous. What began as a small community pet cemetery obviously filled a void the Bay Area desperately needed. Footpaths were abandoned for space, and so there is no clear way into the cemetery, a jumble of stones both standing and in the ground. A section for scattered cremains is fenced off, but the dirt is soft and footing is not secure. In reaching for a pinwheel, somehow my son managed to get a nasty scratch from a bramble bush, and had to be taken back to the car for his wound to be cleaned.

Porkchop – "Our sweet handsome boy" – "If love could have saved you, you would have lived forever – Thank you for all the happiness you brought us"

Leland "World's greatest lap cat"

Muttley "A dog of questionable heritage but unquestionable character."

"We enjoyed all his nine lives"

Like the rest of the Bay Area, Pet's Rest is incredibly diverse. There were stones here in Russian, Chinese, Japanese, Spanish, blessed by priests, registered in "God's care."

Bootsie: "My only son, Love Mommy"

Why can't pets live forever? Or, at least, as long as their owners?

Barbarella: "She asked for so little but gave so much"

The overarching sentiment in the pet cemetery is the power of unconditional love. Our pets give us so much love, companionship, and comfort, and yet ask for so little in return. Their lack of judgment makes them ultimately the perfect object of affection.

Pet cemeteries, like pets themselves, remind us of what makes us human: our ability to care for each other. We may have the chance to encounter several beloved companions in our lifetime, preparing us for the inevitable, teaching us lessons along the way about how wonderful it is to take care of each other, or to allow someone to take care of us.

It comes as no surprise that in addition to being considered a destination in travel guidebooks of the area, Pet's Rest is the most visited cemetery in all of the Colma necropolis.

JAPANESE CEMETERY

On a bed of stones, the bright pink flowers surrounding a small in-ground plaque caught my eye, reminding me of cherry blossoms. Then I noticed the portraits of a handsome young couple, George and Sachi, in the prime of life.

I posted this photo on my Instagram for its beauty but also because I felt it was representative of the Japanese Cemetery as a whole. My heart sank when one follower commented, "They would have been in their 20s during WWII. I hope they didn't get put in one of those awful internment camps."

I couldn't search fast enough. But there it was. I found several records that someone named George S. Ishida had been sent to an internment camp in Arizona and there was some evidence that Sachi had been as well, though I'm not clear where. Approximately 120,000 people of Japanese descent were sent to internment camps after the bombing of Pearl Harbor. The majority were American citizens.

The fact that I didn't consider this given the timing is a source of shame.

The Japanese Cemetery is a shortened name for the Cemetery of the Japanese Benevolent Society. There are benevolent societies all over the Bay Area and in some of the cemeteries in Colma, including the Serbian Cemetery and the Chinese cemeteries. Benevolent societies were founded by Christian (mostly Catholic) churches to help immigrants and the disenfranchised with their needs, including but not limited to employment, health care, and

burial. In New Orleans, Black Americans founded benevolent societies to help people who were frequently turned away from hospitals or doctors because they were Black.

In San Francisco, the Japanese Benevolent Society was founded with a grant from Emperor Meiji, the land for the cemetery purchased, in 1901, for $1,400. Meiji was known as "Meiji the great," and presided over Japan's entry into the world during his reign from 1867 to 1912.

The attack on Pearl Harbor occurred December 7, 1941. As FDR said, it was "a day which will live in infamy." Though there was racism against Asian immigrants before the bombing of Pearl Harbor, discrimination against the Japanese intensified afterward. By 1941 the cemetery was well established as a safe haven for Japanese Americans to bury their loved ones in peace. The racist suspicion of immigrants in the United States, even by the outbreak of World War II, was nothing new. German immigrants and German Americans were also sent to camps during World War I and questioned by the FBI as to where their allegiances stood.

Because of the fact that California is geographically closer to Asia than is the eastern United States, the Asian immigrant population is greater. All of the interment camps of Japanese Americans or those of Japanese descent were in the West. The imprisonment began in 1942 and ended in 1946.

Japanese Americans were fired from their jobs. They lost nearly all their personal property as they could only bring with them what they could carry into the camps. They were barred, in many states, from owning land or homes. In the camps, many died due to lack of proper medical care. Vandalism of Japanese graves and property was frequent. There were reparations made beginning in 1948, but by then the IRS had already destroyed the tax records of those interned. In 1976, President Ford made a public apology that the camps were "a national mistake" and "should never be repeated." The stories of the Japanese people who suffered in these camps are still being uncovered.

Despite these losses, there is no memorial to those who suffered and died in these camps at this cemetery. Simple concrete
blocks near the fence closest to Hillside Boulevard mark the graves
of those who died in internment camps during the war.

During a visit to Japan with my brother, who is a Japanese
translator, we went to Hiroshima, to the Hiroshima Peace Memorial Museum. The one surviving building, its fractured dome,
which resembles a fractured Earth, still stands. In the museum
there are pieces of clothing and human skin taken from those
with radiation after the blast. A group of Japanese schoolchildren
were there, looking at the same piece of bubbled flesh. I will never

forget their faces as they looked up at me, and I looked back down at them.

I told my brother about this as we left the museum. "They probably didn't know you were American," he said.

As we walked though the gardens surrounding the museum, an elderly Japanese man approached us. He spoke English. "Where are you from?" he asked us. "New York," I said. "Thank you so much for coming here," he replied. Then he asked if he could shake our hands.

The day we visited the Japanese Benevolent Society Cemetery there was no one there but the dead. The office was locked up, posted with phone numbers if assistance was required. The graves stood in neat lines, divided into three sections. The plots are scattered with smooth round stones, and a few are planted with withered trees. The office building is partially covered by a large Japanese maple.

At the very front of the cemetery, some of the largest memorials are monuments to white people, including an "Ohio born quaker" named Ernest Sturge M.D. P.H.D., "a spiritual father to us," his epitaph reads, "he loved the Japanese." His monument is the Catholic cross emblazoned with the IHS and surrounded by Japanese kanji. According to *City of Souls*, "beneath the massive memorial are only Sturge's fingernails and hair."

In the newer section, behind the office building, there is a stone for "A-Twice," "a rap artist, and cultural interpreter," a young man and beloved member of the San Francisco community, his life cut short by testicular cancer. Nearby, a triangular monument for two women is adorned with a flaming crouching tiger. On the path back toward the entrance, I found the resting place of Rev. Seiji Kobara, master of the art of shodo calligraphy.

At the very front of the cemetery is a monument perhaps meant to ward off any bad feelings about Japanese-American relations. Erected by the "U.S. Japan Relations Centennial Northern California Japanese Committee on May 15, 1960," three white marble stones gleamed so brightly in the sun it was impossible to read their inscriptions. The central tombstone is a monument to the first Japanese sailor to visit any foreign port. This man and two others died in San Francisco following a "harrowing 37 day voyage from Shinaagawa, Japan" on May 20, 1860.

Just next door is another large rock, a "war memorial tower to the unknown soldier." No specific wars are indicated.

When the cemeteries in San Francisco started to bar new burials and then began the relocation process, many Japanese graves from Laurel Hill and the Masonic Cemetery were moved here. This section is to the right of the entrance, down a long recently paved path. It is marked by a simple tablet that reads, in kanji and in English, "In memory of 107 remains from Laurel Hill Cemetery erected by Calif. Japanese Benevolent Society Oct 1958." Presumably, these remains are all buried beneath this maker or somewhere nearby and are unmarked. The stones that stand behind it are the ones that managed to make it to Colma with the previous occupants of the graves they had marked.

I've never seen this blend of Japanese and Victorian mourning symbolism in the United States: A stately draped mourning urn, with an epitaph completely in kanji, a traditional scroll monument, with the Christ lily and cross, with a Japanese occupant and an epitaph in English. Three incredibly old white tombstones, all in kanji. A monument shaped like a tree stump, its epitaph carved out of its wood in kanji, with a peace dove, olive branch in its mouth.

A leaning tablet with an icon of a hand pointing to the heavens. A large rock monument, marked by cherry blossoms and kanji but with anglicized first names marked by a cross. A broken tombstone, laying against the cemetery's gate, reading "native of Japan, died Feb. 27, 1887."

I took one last look before exiting its gates. It was a lonely-looking place, not neglected— everything was in good shape—but a little forlorn. There

was a big bulletin board, most likely used for community announcements and funerals. But today, it was empty aside from two pieces of paper, one that said, in big black letters, "Please social distance (6ft.) and wear a mask." I took a few more photos and turned to go.

As we waited for the light to change, I saw a dad with his young daughter and their dog out for a walk. Looking over my shoulder as I crossed the street, I watched as they strolled into the cemetery.

GREEK ORTHODOX MEMORIAL PARK AND GREENLAWN MEMORIAL PARK

In order to write this chapter, I've had to break one of journalist Lillian Ross's cardinal rules about reporting: "Do not write about anyone who does not want to be written about."

According to the 1950 San Francisco city report on the removal of cemeteries, residents of Colma asked "what assurance do you have to give us that my plot will not, fifty years from now, be picked up and moved to make way for more densely built-up residential developments?" The trauma from the San Francisco eviction of the cemeteries was so severe that cremation rates rose.

The cemeteries of Colma are understandably protective of their permanent residents. They want to do their best to convince anyone interested in being buried there that their remains will be eternally safe. There is a suspicion—even a litigiousness—from cemetery organizations in the Bay Area, the level of which I have frankly never encountered before. For some of the cemeteries featured in this book, I had to sign a release form before I could enter the grounds. The signage outside Greenlawn, with its emphasis that no photos were allowed, is consistent with the sort of distrust in anyone, journalist or otherwise, who asks questions about the cemeteries in the Bay Area. But I didn't want to leave Greenlawn and Greek Orthodox out of this book, so, despite Lillian Ross's advice, I picked up the phone.

The woman I spoke to, Danae, was friendly and offered to meet with me in person. We set up a time to meet as wildfires raged in Oregon and Northern California. Driving over the Bay Bridge was like driving into a complete whiteout.

Though she was wearing her N-95 mask, Danae smiled and laughed as we commiserated on our love of cemeteries, photography, and writing. I had a hunch that the cemetery was family owned, given the last name of the general manager—Doukas—and

the portrait hanging above Danae's shoulder, of a man named "Nicholas Doukas—Cemetery Founder."

"So, who is this?"

"That's Nick Doukas, the cemetery founder," Danae responded.

"And so, Steve Doukas is . . ."

"His son."

"And Steve Doukas is . . ."

"My dad," Danae smiled.

My assumptions were confirmed. Many cemeteries in the United States began as family businesses, but few remain so. Many have been bought up by larger death service corporations. But the Greek Orthodox Memorial Park was founded by Danae's grandfather in 1934 and is still managed by his son, Steve, and Danae, his granddaughter.

I asked Danae how her grandfather came to the cemetery business, and what he had done before the Greek Orthodox Memorial Park was founded. "I'm not sure," she demurred. But then she said, "Well, I think he saw how the Greek Orthodox were treated at the cemeteries, and he didn't like that."

"So he founded his own," I offered, "He founded his own," she confirmed, as Nick Doukas smiled down at us.

Danae answered my questions and I made sure to let her know she didn't have to respond, or she could speak to me off the record. I asked about a few historical photographs hanging on the wall. "There are other Orthodox cemeteries, certainly," Danae explained, "and burial grounds that belong to churches. But this is the only specifically stand-alone Greek Orthodox cemetery in the U.S." As for the fact that Greenlawn and Greek Orthodox appeared to be under the same no-photography rule, Danae explained, "I manage both cemeteries."

Before we started walking around the grounds, I wanted to ask Danae about the no-photography rule. I wondered if they'd had problems on the grounds with people not respecting the space of mourners, or infractions with family members over photography.

"All of our monuments are privately owned. The family members create them specifically for their loved ones and we just feel it is upsetting to them to see their personal property online," Danae offered. I asked if she had any specific examples. "What do you mean by online," I asked, "like, on social media?" "Exactly," she said, "we feel it could be emotionally damaging to the family members to see their loved one's monument on the Internet."

There was a pause in the conversation.

"If you want to photograph the stones from behind, that's completely fine," Danae reminded me. "So that no names or identifying information can be seen. And the chapel and my grandparents' monument are totally fine. I can show you those."

We left the office and walked over to the spot where Danae's grandparents are buried. She quickly pulled up some weeds and moved a leaf that had blown in front of their crypt. I never move anything when I'm taking photos: even if text is obscured, even if it looks unkempt. I never use filters on my photographs. My goal is to capture to cemetery as is. But this was different for Danae; these are her grandparents.

We went inside the small chapel adjoining the office, which overlooks the Greek Orthodox Memorial Park in front, sloping down the hill to El Camino Real. Danae explained the Byzantine church, and the difference between the Catholic Church and the Orthodox Church. The small, elegant chapel was lined with red carpet that had been so recently cleaned I could still see the vacuum marks.

I snapped a photo of the Byzantine mosaic and noticed a portrait of Christ to the right side of the altar. I remarked to Danae on its beauty. She laughed, "technically that is not in the Byzantine style. Anything that looks realistic isn't Byzantine. But everything in this chapel was donated."

We walked down the path toward the entrance to Greenlawn. My husband and son were sitting in our car. Worried that Danae might find them suspicious, I told her who they were. Normally my husband takes my son around the cemetery, showing him letters and numbers and generally exploring so he can get some fresh air and exercise. But today the air was not so fresh—with hazardous smoke conditions—so they waited in the car. I remarked to Danae that maybe the air quality was improving. "No," she shook her head, "it's just the sun coming out."

We came to a long patch of dirt at the back of the cemetery. Danae explained that there are often questions in the office about why this section is so unkempt. "It's an option for those who want in-ground burial for a lower cost," Danae said, "not everyone understands this." I looked at the makeshift markers, most small plastic plaques or even wooden crosses. There were also a few

tombstones. "Families can bring in those monuments at their own expense, but we reserve the right to remove them."

By that time Danae had basically shown me the major sites of both cemeteries and gone over with me ways in which I could photograph each without capturing any names or identifying information. We walked slowly back to the office and said our

goodbyes. As I passed her again on my way to take some photos of the Greek Orthodox cemetery, I could hear her instructing a groundskeeper that I had permission to photograph. "Don't harass her," she said, laughing. I thanked her again for her time.

The smoke still held over the mountains and in the distance. From the top of the Greek Orthodox hill near the chapel you have an excellent view across El Camino Real to the Italian Cemetery and Eternal Home, one of the Jewish cemeteries. I walked behind the tombstones, taking pictures of the sweeping hill of the Greek Orthodox cemetery with its many crosses and the chapel in the background.

Next to the cemetery is a outdoor crypt. I took a quick sad walk through, thinking of all the people in the mausoleum and in the cemetery whose names I would never know, whose stories I cannot tell you because they are private. There were several photo portraits on the crypts, including one of a young man with wild dark hair and an intense mustache. He looked like a good time. "You wouldn't mind, would you?" I said to him, aloud, "if I took your picture?"

Back through Greenlawn, I walked the whole path from front to back, venturing off from side to side to investigate curious monuments. As I made my way to the very back left corner near the non-endowment care section, the graves changed, from European from the late 1800s to Asian from the early to mid-1900s with incredible photo portraits. There was a young man in his sailor uniform. Another dashing young man, sporting a bow

tie and holding a pipe, right next to a boy who could've been his classmate with a bouffant hairdo. A young woman wearing a mink stole, pearls and glasses gave me a skeptical look from her stone.

A man and his son, who died when he was five years old. A little girl, her stone adorned with lambs, only three. A glamorous woman drenched in white fur with a a flapper haircut and lipstick. Two young girls side by side. An adorable couple's portrait, born the same year; died the same year.

At the very outskirts of this section, there were more portraits. A Black woman with an incredible hat, an affable young man in a suit, an incredibly beautiful Black woman with a glowing smile to match her gold earrings.

How I wish I could share their portraits with you.

TESTAMENT:
JEWISH CEMETERIES OF COLMA

HILLS OF ETERNITY

The most notorious occupant of Hills of Eternity cemetery, the largest Jewish cemetery in Northern California, is not even Jewish. But he was, appropriately, from Tombstone.

Wyatt Earp is known as an iconic lawman, a "good guy." He was played by Kurt Russell in the 1993 film *Tombstone*. His legend has become much larger than the man. The real Wyatt Earp was a gambler, a criminal, and an enterprising businessman. After the shoot-out at the O.K. Corral, in which he evidently oversold his involvement, Earp traveled through the West, eventually ending up in Los Angeles, where he lived with his common-law wife, Josephine, who was Jewish. When he died in 1929, he was "secretly" cremated and buried in Josephine's family plot at Hills of Eternity.

For many years, no one knew the location of Earp's remains. But when people got word he was buried at Hills of Eternity, his grave was vandalized over and over again. His and Josephine's tombstone was stolen four times. The third stone, weighing nearly 300 pounds, was eventually found in a flea market. The fourth and final stone that you see today was set into concrete, making it impossible to remove.

As I arrived at the Hills of Eternity, I set upon my search for Wyatt Earp, wondering how it is that people like him are advanced to such epic proportions. His name is synonymous with the idea of cowboys and shoot-outs. "Who was Wyatt Earp?" my husband asked as we parked in the cemetery. I opened my mouth, then shut it again. Who, indeed? I tried to explain, but could come up with nothing better than the explanation that he was a real person but most of his life had been embellished by the need for a narrative of the Wild West.

Over on the southern side of the cemetery, just at the edge of an older plot, I finally found his stone, with a scroll design bearing his last name. Josephine died in 1944, but not before cementing her image as Earp's official wife (he was apparently still married to a prostitute when they met) with the publication of *I Married Wyatt Earp*, a mostly fictitious account of her time with Earp. Their shared epitaph reads: "... That nothing's so sacred as honor, and nothing so loyal as love!"

The sensationalism of Earp's story stands in stark contrast to the rest of this cemetery, which can only be described as one of the most beautiful places I have ever seen. Just in front of Earp is the obelisk for a man, a native of Prussia, who died in 1880: "A devoted husband, a good father." Coming from the East, I'm accustomed to a much different look in Jewish cemeteries, where most of the monuments are uniform, stately, and rather plain. But Hills of Eternity, Home of Peace, and Salem Memorial Park, all under the same management, are much older. They blend Jewish symbolism with that of the Victorian park cemetery: Hebrew lettering, menorahs, the Star of David, and Cohanim hands cover marble tombstones with draped urns, floral wreaths, scrolls, ferns, ornate mausolea, weeping willows, rosebuds, and more. Taking a walk through these cemeteries is like taking a course in the history of typography. "Wow," one person commented on an Instagram post of a particularly ornate stone, "they used every font."

Like many pioneers, Jews were drawn to the Bay Area because of the Gold Rush beginning in 1849. Those who were in the States on the eastern side of the country traveled West in hopes of striking it rich. These immigrants were already familiar with American customs and with the English language, so they thrived in the West, building communities in the Jewish faith, with synagogues, orphanages, and cemeteries. Anti-Semitism was not so prevalent in the West before and during the Gold Rush, though this would change.

On average, I shoot between 100 and 200 photographs when I visit a cemetery for the first time. I took nearly 400 photos during my first visit to Hills of Eternity. Practically every corner, every plot, every single stone is worth photographing. It's an embarrassment of riches.

When Emanuel Hart Cemetery in San Francisco became full in 1860, land was purchased at what is now Mission Dolores Park for Home of Peace. "Unquestionably it became San Francisco's most prestigious burial ground," according to *City of Souls*. But as we know, it was not to last. Unfortunately with urbanization and gentrification there is often a rise in racism. Whether the move was an anticipation of their eviction, or as a result of "Anti-Semitic vandalism," as Michael Svanevik has suggested, Home of Peace was moved to Colma by 1900. San Francisco, which had been a freewheeling community of pioneers, was now becoming an established urban center of commerce.

One young woman's obelisk contains a mirror-shaped plaque with her names, dates, and epitaph, a beloved daughter who died at just 25. Adorned with daffodils, symbolizing the death of a young person, this incredible piece of artwork is topped with a full bouquet of roses, the symbol of the death of a young woman. And underneath, just above a concrete slab, this moving epitaph: "Betsy, parents and friends your absence mourn, even in death your virtues still do live. Into eternity thy spirit is bourne, saddened hearts, to thee true sympathy give, ever rests thy spirit still on those with whom remembrances of thee, make an altar of thy tomb."

A marble bust portrait of a young woman named Natalie, "lost on steamer," was impossible to ignore, her long ringlets beaming in the sunlight.

My husband and son had been wandering around Home of Peace on their own, reading letters and numbers off stones. I remarked that this place was much larger than I expected and that we would need to return. My husband agreed. "I think this is my favorite one," he said quietly.

"Look, Mama," my son yelled, pointing in the distance, "a star!"

There was a domed mausoleum with a large Star of David in the center of it. "Yes, great job," I told him, "that is a star! That's the Jewish star, the Star of David."

"Jewish star," he echoed.

Just next to this mausoleum was another, quite large, equally imposing. We rounded the corner to the footpath. "Oh," I said, feeling stupid. "Duh." It was the Levi Strauss mausoleum. It had been on my list of things to see at Home of Peace, but I had been distracted by the beauty of the grounds.

"Can we go in?" my son asked.

Levi Strauss is best known as the creator of blue jeans. Strauss had owned a dry goods store and wanted to make stronger work pants, so he tried denim. They became so popular he opened a factory in San Francisco and was made a millionaire. Born in Germany, his family had immigrated to the United States when he

was 18. As one of the most successful businessmen in the Bay Area, Strauss was a dedicated philanthropist to the Jewish community, establishing the first Jewish synagogue in San Francisco.

The mausoleum is a tribute to his mother, who died in 1869. Her marble bust appears at the top center of the crypt above the inscription "Our Mother," guarded by two robed women and a small child. Rumor has it the bust was designed by Auguste Rodin.

There were some unbelievable monuments at the edge of the cemetery's land. Just next door, an auto shop was in operation, washing cars outside, blasting the radio. I passed one tomb topped with a woman bearing an urn or a vase, covered in Hebrew. But at the bottom there was English: "Sacred to the memory of a widowed mother, who to her children was father and mother both."

I was blessed with one last showstopping stone. The Figels—
Isabel "called" in 1901, and Joseph "followed" in 1908. Their
shared gravestone is draped with an incredible tasseled curtain.
A bouquet of two different kinds of leaves, one unidentified for
Isabel and an acanthus for Joseph, bound by a bow centers their

epitaphs, chiseled in English and Hebrew. The carving work on this stone and its near-pristine condition made it pop out of the green grass and the bright blue sky as if some kind of heavenly spotlight illuminated it.

HOME OF PEACE

I had barely made a dent in Home of Peace, and so we returned to get a better sense of the place. Home of Peace and Hills of Eternity share an office, and are only separated by the central road through the cemetery. There was an obvious mausoleum row, a circle of large crypts. One for Albert Abrams, an Egyptian Revival

mausoleum with a winged sun disk flanked by two cobras, its columns and ornate bronze door engraved with lotus flowers, is guarded by two puggish sphinxes.

Around the corner from the Abrams mausoleum, there was a beautiful fountain and at its center several large Stars of David, directly in front of the Goldman mausoleum.

To my left a monolithic crypt loomed—the resting place of Joseph Naphtaly, the legal counsel for the congregation. Also in the Egyptian Revival style, according to *City of Souls*, the "stone atop the vault weighs 20 tons." The mausolea on this circular drive

surrounding the fountain were mostly built at the turn of the twentieth century, and yet, because of the hard work of the cemetery's grounds crew, they looked brand-spanking new.

An unusual monument caught my eye as I crossed back to the main path that divides Hills of Eternity and Home of Peace. This is the Meyerfield memorial, emblazoned with a quotation from "An Elegy on the Death of John Keats," by his friend Percy Bysshe Shelley: "He has outsoared the shadow of our night."

Back on the Hills of Eternity side, there was a tombstone still wrapped in plastic, ready for an unveiling ceremony. In the Jewish tradition the stone marker is only revealed in the first year after death, and loved ones gather at the grave to recite prayers. This veiled monument is the resting place of George "Jorge" Rosenkrantz, "creator of the birth control pill, passionate innovator, compassionate humanist." I stood there in respect and appreciation for George Rosencrantz, and I thought of his family, too. "Loving husband, dedicated father, beloved grandfather. A bright light to guide us all."

George was born in Hungary in 1916, and just a few steps down the row were gorgeous tombstones of families dating back as early as 1880, natives of Prussia, Poland, and New York. Another stone with unusual typeface bore a simple message that was like a punch to the gut: "Your family loves you and misses your smile."

A few rows from George Rosencrantz was another remarkable Jewish man, whose epitaph made me smile: Alexander Garay: "devoted husband, loving father, caring brother and inspirational grandfather. A courageous Holocaust survivor, fighter and true mensch. Always creative and stylish, making an extraordinary life for himself and his family. Brave and determined to the end he reminds us 'Garays don't give up' - Czech - Israel - NYC - SF. Too well loved to be forgotten." Alexander was born in 1921. I like to think that maybe he and George could have been friends.

All too often cemeteries are seen as depressing, gloomy places. I was having such an incredible time at Hills of Eternity and Home of Peace, reading about the lives of these people, many of them survivors, who faced the ultimate evil and made a success of their lives, even doing so with a sense of humor! Like Ruth and Phillip. Phillip's epitaph reads "I did it my way." Ruth's says, "That's what he thinks."

At the back of the cemetery, there was a large section of older tombstones, mostly from the late 1880s. It's safe to assume these make up the large number that were moved from San Francisco before the cemeteries were evicted from the city. Many of these Jewish people were born in Germany or Poland and died in San Francisco in the last decade of the 1800s. Their stones bear the mourning imagery that was popular in the Victorian period: flora and fauna—lilies, roses, weeping willows, urns, doves, clasped hands, their epitaphs in English and in Hebrew. An ancient post bearing a plaque that read: "Plot P Sec 2 / Row 1 Graves 1-48" proved there was an organization at some point.

A stone for Hanchen Levy listed her birth and death dates in both the Western and the Jewish calendar. 1844 (5604)–1878 (5638).

The spectacular craftsmanship of these tombstones was obvious. Some nearly 150 years old, they still looked unbelievably beautiful. These pioneer stones are a testament to the strong Jewish immigrant community that made the Bay Area their home. In an infant section graves dating back to the 1840s intermingle with those from as recent as 2008. "Our joy will be greater, our love will be deeper, our life will be fuller, because we shared your moment." One tombstone for a little girl listed her date of birth, her date of adoption, and her date of death, just one year later, in both Hebrew and kanji, "forever loved by her forever family."

Rounding back to the entrance, on the far side of Hills of Eternity, there was a newer section with incredibly large marble slab tombstones with engraved portraits, and gold leaf lettering, many of the names in Cyrillic, some with marble sculpted busts of the deceased, extremely impressive to say the least. A giant menorah, blazing with light. Another tombstone in the shape of a piano, with a musical quotation carved into the granite.

I came upon one of the most striking and unusual graves I've ever seen, the resting place of Soviet actor Savely Kramarov. A popular comic actor during the 1960s and 1970s, Kramarov was

born in Moscow and appeared in forty-two Soviet films. Upon attempting to emigrate to the United States in 1979, his career was destroyed by the USSR. When he was finally allowed to leave in 1981, he was considered a traitor and enemy by the Kremlin, and returned to Russia only once in 1992. He was just beginning to rehabilitate his acting career here in America when he died of complications from surgery when he was sixty.

Other immigrants who had been similarly treated by the former Soviet Union raised money to install this memorial for Kramrov here at Hills of Eternity. Built to look like an actor's dressing room table, it contains makeup brushes, Kramarov's comedy masks, scripts, and a framed photograph of the actor. Embedded into the back brick wall of the theater dressing room, is a skull, a reference, perhaps to poor Yorick—a fitting tribute to an actor, indeed.

SALEM MEMORIAL
Hills of Eternity, Home of Peace, and Eternal Home are all part of the same congregation and under the same management in Colma. Salem stands on its own, but inextricable from the unbelievable Jewish memorial in the necropolis. Salem means peace.

Slightly smaller than the other three cemeteries, Salem is no less beautiful. When we arrived, the hydrangeas were in full bloom. They stood in a color explosion, in bright pinks and purples, full enough to appear as if they were supporting the tombstones they surrounded. Wedged between the tombstones of Gertrude and Margaret, they seemed both interloper and guardian.

The sentimental Victorian mourning symbolism is all here: the clasped hands, urns, weeping willows, rosebuds, unbelievable floral wreaths, scrolls to rival those of Moses. The typography used on the tombstones is enough to keep scholars busy for years. We were alone, once again, in the cemetery. There were no other people aside from one groundskeeper, who clasped his hat to me in greeting as he returned to his car at the back at the cemetery. I wanted to yell, "you are doing amazing work," but he knew. His smile said all it needed to say.

More hydrangeas. Looking back at my photos from the day, it is an exercise in framing. First I notice the hydrangeas, bright pink, peering over a set of three family graves like an exquisite garland. I snap a photo from the path. Then, an accidental shot of my feet appear as my excitement in getting closer mounts. The next two shots are blurry. I try to take one in between the graves that sit in front of this family plot. It doesn't work. I go closer. This is the shot. The fog in the back is the perfect gray. The hydrangeas are performing now. The family trio of names: Abraham, Mother, Isabella. A shaft of sunlight lies on the grass in front, dappled with little daisies. It is perfect.

Another symbol I noticed again and again at Salem was the fern. For Annie and her husband Abraham, fern fronds decorate the base of their tombstones. Ferns symbolize a victory over death, but more importantly a sincerity, indicating a person of honesty. Another fern monument across the path for a woman named Elizabeth who died at age thirty-eight includes the epitaph: "I believe that I have done some good in this world."

ETERNAL HOME

We were wrapping up our many weekends spent in Colma. After a quick calculation, I realized we'd spent every weekend since April here, about twenty weeks. Eternal Home was the last cemetery to see. From the street, it's just next to the Italian Cemetery. The large Holocaust memorial is clearly visible from the road, buttressed by uniform tombstones on every side, a plaque with many names topped by a large menorah. "This monument is dedicated in memory of the six million Jews who perished in the Holocaust, erected by the Holocaust survivors to remember forever those who perished during the Nazi reign of terror."

As I snapped a few photos, there was a small group of people gathered by one of the tombstones near the street. They gradually made their way up the hill and stood chatting on the road. None of them were wearing masks. I pulled mine up and wanted to get

quickly out of their way in respect for their mourning, trying to make my way back to the car without disturbing them.

An older man standing closest to me asked me something but I didn't quite hear him and asked him to repeat himself. "Are you Jewish?" he said. "No," I shook my head. He smiled. "Are you a photographer?" I paused, not sure what to say. I nodded with a muffled yes from behind my face mask. The women standing near him looked over in my direction, sizing me up. "Have a nice day," I said. Reaching to open the car door I heard him reply, giving me the thumbs-up, "important work!"

As soon as we drove through its gates, I noticed the cemetery was much larger than I expected. As we came up the hill, it unfolded, split in half by the road, all the way back to El Camino Real. We parked on the side of the road and I looked to my right. There was a large patch of tall sunflowers—a sunflower farm—right next to the cemetery. I took off immediately, with only one arm in my jacket, ran down a small hill, and looked up into the sunflowers. My son struggled at the top of the hill, wanting to catch up with me, shrieking about the flowers, my husband following behind him.

This part of the cemetery is much older than the section visible from the street. Jewish symbols blended with Victorian mourning symbols, the draped urn, the scroll, ferns, weeping willows, with Hebrew and English epitaphs. "Native of Germany, died 1907."

There were a few mausolea next to the road and a complete row at the back of the section behind the office. Approaching from behind, I saw that the stained glass window was a beautiful rendition of a menorah, set against the Star of David. The front of the mausoleum revealed a gorgeous marbleized reddish gray granite with an ornate bronze door. Inside, the Star of David was bright blue and outlined in red. On the windowpane, there were several family photographs and stones, even a portrait of a beloved family dog.

Cohanim hands, which symbolize the priestly blessing, greeted me on many stones. There were many beloved grandmothers: the back of one's gravestone simply read: Oma. "Her children rise up, and call her blessed."

Two grandparents had lengthy epitaphs on the back of their tombstones: "Life was good to her and she was good to life . . . Loved and Remembered, Always Bubie." Many stones, like these, were topped with an open book, the Book of Life. "Look at all the books!" my son shouted.

A large tablet stone with a shorter one just next to it caught my eye. Its epitaph was plainly amazing: "Eugenia Helena Chanarina Sternlight, Native of Poland, Occupation Protective Name Helena Czugalinksa, Called by all and known as Zenia, Underground Fighter Against the Nazis in the Years 1939–1945, Born on April 2, 1901, Departed on September 11, 1965, My Dear Wife."

The shorter stone belonged to her husband: "Jacob Sternlight, Native of Poland, Jan 10, 1905–June 12, 1977, Beloved Brother and Uncle."

Jacob had thought the world of Zenia to establish this monument for her, much taller than his own. I thanked him and Zenia, as I looked around this place, thinking of the survivors of the Holocaust and those who had fought, like Zenia, against fascism.

The closer I got to the front of the cemetery the more the stones began to look like what I was more accustomed to seeing in Jewish cemeteries on the East Coast, very uniform, dark granite, shaped similarly with white inscriptions and simple ornamentation like the Star of David or a menorah. There weren't many

portraits on the older stones, excepting for one, a striking woman named Rose, who smiled up at me from her beautiful stone.

I had stumbled into the children's section at Eternal Home. One grave for a little girl who died just after her first birthday was covered in stuffed animals and fresh flowers. An epitaph for a little boy who died just before his first birthday moved me to tears: "Brilliant Smile, Sparkling Eyes, Indomitable Spirit." One incredible family monument, a trio of heart-shaped graves, for parents and their children in between made sure not to forget Baby David who died at barely three months.

Another epitaph for an infant was hard to make out, covered in lichen "...truth to say she had not grown up but gone away and it is but a child of air that lingers in the garden there."

A group of seven little tombstones, all for babies or small children, sat grouped together in a particularly muddy patch. One could assume there's been some damage to this area, and perhaps the cemetery felt it best to move them closer together for structural support.

Another small heart-shaped tombstone: "Our Darling Dollbaby."

A few days before our visit to Eternal Home there had been an intense thunderstorm. Rain in the Bay Area at this time of year is extremely unusual, much less a storm with thunder and lightning. A neighbor who has lived in the East Bay for forty years said, "I can't remember the last time I heard thunder." Another said the thunder woke him, and he just assumed it was an earthquake. Weather authorities believe that the lightning is what may have ignited the forest fires that were still raging several weeks later.

Under a lone tree there were beautiful tombstones covered in a giant branch that had fallen, spraying leaves and broken twigs

around the area. The work trucks were out in the distance clearing debris.

In the long view toward the mountains with the morning fog still hanging in the air, the tombstones stared back at me, a sea of faces like the bright sunflower patch to my right. Sunflowers are an unusual symbol for gravestones—if you do see them, according to cemetery symbolism expert Doug Keister, they are usually on Catholic graves, as sunlight represents god and the sunflower the striving toward God. Before Colma was the city of the dead, it was farmland for lettuce, cabbage, and later, flowers, thanks to moisture from the fog and fertile, swampy soil. It's likely that these flowers have been here longer than the cemetery, growing and striving to turn their faces to the sun.

PART III

CONTRA COSTA

THE EAST BAY

THE CHAPEL OF THE CHIMES, OAKLAND

The plan for the day was to visit Mountain View Cemetery, and then head over to the Chapel, just a few feet away. We tentatively approached the entrance gates to Mountain View. Immediately I saw the large traffic cones. I got out of the door and approached the security guard, who greeted me atop of a motorized scooter. "Can I help you?" He eyed me suspiciously. I explained that I was working on a book and wanted access to the cemetery for research purposes.

"Well, the cemetery is closed to the public. I don't know about all that," he said, presumably meaning my book, "you can try and call the number."

"Oh well," I said to my husband, "let's try for the chapel." A friendly staff member asked us if we were here for the service—there was a funeral going on—and when we replied if we could just see the mausoleum, he obliged. "Oh yes, the mausoleum is open, go straight through there."

As soon as I walked through the doors of the Chapel of the Chimes, all my frustrations over Mountain View's inaccessibility evaporated.

"Wow," I said. "Gorgeous!"

"Wow," my son echoed, "gorgeous!"

We scurried down to the entrance toward the mausoleum. It felt like we were in a smaller version of the dining hall at Hogwarts, with elegant Gothic style arches and stained glass skylights. Each room reveals endless shelves of gold and brown book urns behind glass niches. In the center of most of the rooms, there are running fountains and green plantings. One man's niche was adorned with a hanging charm of paper cranes, American flags, and plastic sushi keychains. Many of the cubbies contain personal mementos and photographs of the deceased. And the rooms keep coming.

The skylights make it feel as if you're outside with plenty of light in the main hallway. But as you venture farther back into the mausoleum, the light dims. The day we visited it was extremely hot and humid. The air inside wasn't moving, and the face mask I was sporting didn't help. After entering a room and taking photographs, I frequently had to pull down my face mask and wipe the sweat off my face. My husband decided the lack of air circulation was not a good idea in terms of Covid-19, so he and my son went to wait outside while I continued on.

While I was inside the Chapel of the Chimes I only saw three other people. One woman was departing just as I was entering. She held a handkerchief over her face and was visibly crying. Another couple was chatting about the mausoleum's beauty while

the woman took photographs with a professional-looking camera. "I always post these to Redbubble," she said to her companion, "they do really well."

Every room held an overwhelming amount of visual stimuli. Inside large mausoleums like this one, I go into sensory overload, wanting to capture everything, remember everything. I skulked to the side, shamed by the woman's clunky big camera, fingering my measly iPhone, and noticed the back of one column of urns was visible. On the back, there were labels: the name of the crematory, the name of the deceased, the date of birth, death, and cremation.

An odd plaque commemorated "Col. Henry Laurens, first president of the Continental Congress, 1774, first caucasian cremated in North America, Charleston S.C. 1792." So the Chapel of the Chimes is not only a columbarium, it is a celebration of the act of cremation itself.

There was a column labeled "Lullabyland." From its bronze vases hung baby's breath and a small yellow bear. "Lullabyland," in cemetery parlance, refers to the graves of small children, usually infants. In the corner was a small room with a sink, presumably for washing out vases and flowers. Even the sink, with blue striped tile, was pretty.

The Chapel of the Chimes was built in 1909, but it underwent a significant addition and refurbishment by the architect Julia Morgan in 1928. Julia Morgan is best known as the designer of San Simeon, otherwise known as Hearst Castle, the gargantuan luxury palace she built for William Randolph Hearst. It is plainly ridiculous, an American Versailles—but it includes some of the most beautiful architecture of the 20th century. My personal favorite is the outdoor checkered pool. I specify outdoor pool because there is also an insane indoor pool, a sparkling blue mosaic grotto.

Julia Morgan is unique for her designs, but she is also unique because of her gender. Morgan was the first woman to earn her architecture license in the state of California. She designed more

than 700 buildings in her career, many for UC Berkeley, and all over the Bay Area, pioneering the use more stable materials, like reinforced concrete, after many buildings were damaged by the 1906 earthquake. She was born in San Francisco, attended Berkeley, and died in San Francisco. She never married and was intensely private. She is buried at Mountain View Cemetery, across the street.

As I walked through the halls of the Chapel of the Chimes, I realized Morgan was hard at work on this project and Hearst Castle at the same time. She was hired in 1926 for the Chimes and finished it in 1928. Hearst hired her for San Simeon in 1919 and it wasn't completed until 1947.

Because of the many book-shaped urns in the Chapel of the Chimes—there are thousands and thousands—it is sometimes referred to as "the library of souls." It is an appropriate moniker. Looking at photos of the largest rooms, you almost forget that you're looking at volumes of people: each one with a life, a story, a family, and a legacy.

The blend of the natural world with its inevitable, permanent end makes the Chapel of the Chimes into a place of light and hope when it could be dark and foreboding. I rounded a corner and found a large green tree growing straight out of the ground with two small cages underneath. There were living birds, chirping away, in the middle of the mausoleum. One was yellow, the other a vibrant orange. A small plaque explained that the birds were well cared for by the staff and gave a number if any concerns should arise. "Hi," I said to the yellow bird. "Look at you!" He cocked his head at me, probably wondering if I had any snacks.

Similar to the mausoleum to end all mausoleums, the Great Mausoleum, at Forest Lawn, in Los Angeles, the Chapel of the Chimes also offers Christian ethos on its walls: Commit Thy Way Unto the Lord, Walk in Love, one reads. A statue of an angel with gorgeous blue ombre mosaic wings awaits you patiently, its arms cross in

front in supplication. Bible verses and mosaics portraying events from the Old Testament proclaim themselves.

I had now entered the mausoleum part of the mausoleum, meaning I was in the wall crypt section—where the caskets are slid into the wall and covered with a marble slab. One favorite

epitaph of the day was for a man named Frank. It read simply, "Love you babe, Wanda."

There was no sound, the air unmoving, aside from the trickle from the fountains and a random peep from the birds in the next room.

Back in another niche room, the books of a couple were accompanied by their youthful portrait. They were both blond, and she was wearing pearls. Another perplexing plaque read: "Immortal Love, Forever Full, Forever Flowing Free, Forever Shared, Forever Whole, a Never Ebbing Sea ..."

One wall crypt had another white couple looking like the Cleavers on *Leave It to Beaver*. He was wearing his Navy uniform. Her epitaph read, "Housewife. Nurse." There was a black paper with something written on it underneath. I got closer to read:

Some of the most important lessons I have learned in my life:

To expect good to come to me
To be optimistic
To be self-reliant
To be independent
To have courage
To be strong and healthy
To have guts and spark
To live and let live
To have self-respect
To avoid complaining
To mind my own business
To enjoy life
To try to be unbelievably kind
To just be good
To try to be the best I can be
To not be miserable
To not gossip
To try to be neat and clean
To be true to myself

It was signed by the deceased. I looked up at her portrait. I thought it was nice that she wanted to impart some knowledge, to be useful, in her parting words.

By this point the style of the mausoleum had changed— things were much larger, mostly marble. The next room revealed what appeared to be an even-newer section. One room with mostly Chinese names had featured panel with a bronze depiction of the Statue of Liberty with the quotation, "Here they found life because here there was freedom to live." Eyebrows raised, I was surprised to find it was attributed to Franklin Delano Roosevelt.

I could feel a slight breeze, and to my delight, a door was open on to a terrace. On my way out the door I saw two very unusual wall crypts, one with a gigantic photograph of the deceased who looked like a Bond villain that had just stepped off his yacht. Just next to him was another portrait—a total surprise—the resting place of Blues legend John Lee Hooker. His epitaph read "King of the Boogie," and included his signature in cursive, in which fans had tucked guitar picks, shells, and playing cards.

I went outside. The sky looked ominous. There were nice large concrete beds with trees and in some of them, niches for cremains. I peeked over the edge at the parking lot and in the distance I could see the many stones of Mountain View. I snapped a photo and shook my head in frustration at not being able to get over there.

Back inside, my husband texted that we were running out of time on toddler schedule. I went back to the front of the mauso-leum, taking as many photos as I could, but I took a wrong turn, and ended up in a small room with a tiny chapel inside. There was a memorial to a young man on the wall who had died in 2012. He was handsome and smiling in his portrait. Later research revealed he had been killed in a motorcycle accident.

By this time I was really hot, and tired of wearing my face mask. I hadn't seen a single other human for nearly an hour but I still wore it, determined to be as safe as possible. Would I ever find the exit? Would we ever get out of this mess? On top of every-thing, I had to use the restroom. "Where are you?" another text buzzed in my hand.

One particularly beautiful room looked cool, in the shady part of the building, but the air was stifling, almost solid. I looked up, "In patience possess ye your souls," the wall reminded me. I'd found my way back out to the main hallway. The memorial service was about to begin. I could see staff members of the Chapel gath-ering toward the front, all wearing black face masks. They nodded at me as I made my way to exit, obviously not dressed for a funeral.

I found my husband and son sitting outside on a bench near the driveway. "We'd better get out of here," he said, "look at the sky." It was black.

About three minutes after we'd gotten into the car and pulled out of the parking lot, the sky broke open in a torrential downpour. For the Bay Area, this was very unusual. It hardly ever rains, much less pours. Thunderstorms are incredibly rare.

THE VIEW FROM HERE

Just near the stately mausolea of Millionaires' Row at Mountain View Cemetery, on a hot, sunny morning in Oakland, I spotted a beautiful mausoleum with an unusual name: Wintermute. It caught my eye for the window at its back, revealing the silhouette of a monument placed on the other side, a grieving woman, head in her hand. The Wintermute mausoleum was put up for sale in 2003 by its occupants' descendant, a man named John W. Schieffler, for $250,000. "It is a way to raise needed funds for the living,"

Schieffler told the *New York Times*. "This whole dilemma has been most distasteful. But one has to live."

Schieffler's grandfather, George Preston Wintermute, built the mausoleum when his teenage son died. According to the *Times*, it houses the remains of George, George Jr., "Mr. Schiffeler's grandmother, Ida Lucille Culver; his aunts Emily Jane and Jeanne Culver Wintermute; and Aunt Jeanne's friend Marie. It also contains Mr. Schiffeler's father, Carl, an opera singer and the son of a German baron, who died when Mr. Schiffeler was a toddler, and his mother, Marjorie Wintermute, a European-tutored painter who met her husband in 1938 while he was singing Wotan's Farewell in 'Ride of the Valkyries.'" Eight people.

Schieffler had planned to reinter his family members at a different cemetery closer to his home in Carmel if he had an interested buyer, but Mountain View stepped in. Family members don't have the legal authority to disinter the occupants and resell the mausoleum. In order to sell a mausoleum or a plot at Mountain View, they have to be empty. These rules vary from state to state and cemetery to cemetery, but at Mountain View, them's the breaks. Schieffler eventually gave up on selling the mausoleum, claiming the cost of moving the bodies was prohibitive. Standing in front of the mausoleum, none of the drama was apparent. It was simply another beautiful tomb with an incredible view. But Schieffler's conundrum presents a common attitude: one that promotes the needs of the living over those of the dead. His hope to sell the mausoleum also raises questions about who has control over what remains.

The Wintermute mausoleum is technically not on Millionaires' Row, the "Who's Who" of San Francisco and the Bay Area. The family mausolea that occupy this path at the top of Mountain View with the incredible vista of the city are the movers and shakers of imperial San Francisco: bankers, founders, businessmen like Domingo Ghirardelli and Dr. Samuel Merritt.

Merritt, mayor of Oakland and founder of its first savings bank, rests in a mausoleum on the coveted large corner lot of Millionaires' Row. Many a street and place in the Bay Area are named for Merritt, including Lake Merritt in Oakland. According to mausoleum expert Douglas Keister, though, despite the fact that Merritt was trained as a physician, he didn't take very good care of himself, dying in 1890 of "diabetes complicated by uremic poisoning" and weighing 340 pounds. This larger-than-life person has the mausoleum to match, fashioned as a miniature Mausoleum of Halicarnassus, one of the Seven Wonders of the Ancient World.

The ornate bronze door leaves space above so that one can peak into the vestibule, but the windows on either side were boarded up. A bronze plaque on its front erected by the staff of the Samuel

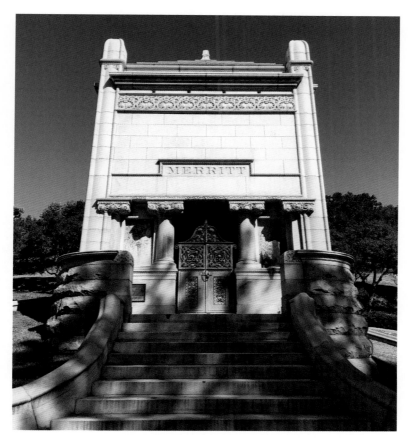

Merritt Hospital lists Merritt's many achievements. Underneath the boarded-up window on the right, there were dozens of spent tea candles and two larger broken saints' candles. The wax had dripped down the front of the granite ledge.

Just down the path from Merritt is the Ghirardelli mausoleum, the resting place of the famous chocolatier Domingo Ghirardelli and his family. But Ghirardelli is infamous at Mountain View for another reason. According to the *San Francisco Chronicle*, Domingo was enraged when his teenage granddaughter Aurelia became ill and was denied last rites by the priest. The reasons

behind this are uncertain: some say the priest was drunk, or that he was delayed by inclement weather, or that perhaps that he didn't feel Domingo had given enough money to the church. For whatever reason, Aurelia died without the administration of last rites and was buried just next to Mountain View, at St. Mary's Catholic Cemetery in the Ghirardelli family plot.

Furious, Domingo forbade any surviving members of his family to ever set foot in a Catholic church again. Then he took matters into his own hands, exhuming his daughter and transferring her and three other family members from the Catholic St. Mary's to a new mausoleum he had just built at Mountain View by horse-drawn carriage under the cover of night. This mausoleum bears the Freemason symbol, which is strictly forbidden by Catholics, which was no doubt intentionally included by Domingo. Domingo joined his family in this mausoleum when he died in 1894.

There are several other beautiful mausolea here just next to the Ghirardelli family, including the Miller mausoleum, one of two pyramid mausolea here at Mountain View. C. O. G. Miller was a founder of the Pacific Lighting Corporation whose unusually-named wife, Einnim, died tragically at the age of 30 in 1896. Miller built this Egyptian Revival mausoleum for her and it bears her likeness in a bust on the front door with her nickname, "Enie" at the top. As I peeked inside the mausoleum, an empty crypt just next to Enie's bore a small bouquet of fake white flowers.

I had an overwhelming sense of déjà vu. I had been to Mountain View twice before, but both trips were extremely short. Regardless, I felt I knew it well. Mountain View is very much like the other park cemeteries that inspired it: Green-Wood Cemetery, in Brooklyn, and Mount Auburn Cemetery, in Cambridge, Massachusetts, both of which were inspired by Père Lachaise, in Paris. All of these cemeteries conform to the park or "rural" cemetery plan, created by the Victorians, which prioritizes the natural landscape, making the cemetery a place for recreation and rumination. Green-Wood was so popular with the living that it made New York City realize its need for a recreational green space. Thus, Central Park—and the modern city park—were born. Frederick Law Olmsted, Central Park's designer, who had headed West for a mining estate job, was engaged to design Mountain View Cemetery. In the 1920s, his son, Frederick Law Olmsted, Jr., would continue his work at the cemetery. Like Green-Wood and Mount Auburn, Mountain View is gorgeous.

The "Millionaires' Row" at Mountain View has many progenitors in the mausolea at Green-Wood, at Mount Auburn, contemporaries at Woodlawn Cemetery, in the Bronx, and descendants in later park cemeteries all over the United States. With the rapid development of American cities, the park cemeteries are often the only remaining public green space, when city parks, botanical gardens, zoos, and playgrounds are frequently crowded or charge admission for entry. Mountain View, like other public park cemeteries, can be a safe haven in chaotic times. This was certainly the case at Mountain View in the early days of lockdown during the pandemic. Residents of the Bay Area knew they could rely on Mountain View as a place to take socially distanced walks, to get some fresh air. Before the lockdown, the first time I visited Mountain View I was struck by the public's use of this cemetery. People were everywhere: walking, jogging, some in small groups, talking on their phones, friends chatting, walking their dogs, sitting by the fountain. My husband had to drive carefully in order to avoid the many pedestrians and other cars. There was a funeral going on at the front of the cemetery, and I could see the casket waiting to be lifted into an outdoor wall crypt, covered in lilies. There was *traffic*.

My goal in writing *Silent Cities* is not only to uncover the history of cemeteries like Mountain View, but to promote cemeteries as places of meditation and to show how essential they are to the living. Apparently, everyone in Oakland got the memo.

When I started my fieldwork for this book I was relieved to be close to Mountain View and I looked forward to covering every inch of the cemetery. Then, the entire Bay Area was placed on lockdown due to Covid-19. I was horrified to learn that Mountain View was closed to the public. I called and pleaded my case. I told them I was writing a book about cemeteries in the Bay Area, but was denied access. Surely, this wouldn't last long, I told myself. Weeks passed.

Weeks turned into months. After a trip to the Chapel of the Chimes, which is right next door, I thought the cemetery would have reopened. But the signs were still up that the cemetery was closed to visitors. After more time had passed and Mountain View remained closed, I didn't have a choice. So I emailed the president, Jeff Lindeman. He was apologetic about the situation and recommended that I meet with Kristie Ly, Mountain View's Customer Service Manager.

The gates opened. I was back. Kristie led me to a small room off the main office desk. We were both wearing our face masks and we were separated by a plastic partition. I listened as she explained Mountain View's decision to close to the public. After lockdown, parks and playgrounds and other recreation like hiking trails were closed in the Bay Area to encourage people to stay home. As a result, attendance at the already popular cemetery went up. People became more and more desperate for fresh air and the outdoors.

"There were hundreds of people standing outside our gates each morning," Kristie said. "Most not wearing masks, since back then we thought masks were useless." There is only one bathroom at Mountain View, and that is in the main office. "We had to close the office off because there were hundreds of people trying to use the restroom. It just wasn't working," Kristie explained. "We had to protect our staff members. The last straw was when we closed the restroom. People started doing their business on cemetery grounds."

Despite the fact that it is an essential part of the community here in the East Bay, at the end of the day, Mountain View is a cemetery, and the families that have loved ones buried here are the priority. As I write this, Mountain View remains closed to the public. "We are, like everyone else, playing it by ear with Covid," Kristie said, shaking her head. When she learned I have a young son, she mentioned all the events that Mountain View usually provides to the community: trick-or-treating, pictures with Santa, Easter egg hunts, all of which were canceled during the pandemic.

I had heard much of the same problems from Green-Wood Cemetery, back in Brooklyn. It was similarly mobbed after lock-down began, so much so that President Richard Moylan had to send out a letter pleading with people to respect the rules or the cemetery would have to close. So much of my first book, *Silent Cities New York*, is about the fact that cemeteries are undervalued by society. My chapter on Green-Wood is about its stillness, its beauty, and its quiet. It is difficult for me to even imagine the cemetery crowded with people, especially people climbing trees, riding bicycles, letting their dogs pee on tombstones, trashing graves and strewing garbage.

"You know, we are open every day," Kristie said. "Our office is open every day, even Thanksgiving, Christmas. Death doesn't take a holiday. Covid has shown us that we have taken Mountain View for granted. It's a privilege to be able to be open to the public."

Kristie was giving me special permission to walk the cemetery grounds because of this book. "You'll be the only person out there today," she said, smiling. "If the grounds staff gives you any trouble, tell them they can call me in the office." Kristie went back to work, in the bustling office, and I stepped outside. It was hot; already eighty-four degrees and barely noon.

There was a large construction project at the outdoor crypts just behind the first fountain, blocked off and encircled by metal fencing. If you aren't open to the public, as many places have discovered during lockdown, it is a good idea to get some repairs done.

I ambled over toward the lawn beyond the crypts, it was bright green and perfectly kept. The mausoleum to the right beckoned me, but I had limited time and I wanted to find Julia Morgan, the

architect of the Chapel of the Chimes and Hearst Castle and of so many buildings in the Bay Area. "You won't be too impressed with her grave," Kristie had warned. "It's just a plain stone with all her family members' names."

Under a gigantic tree rest Ira and Mansie Condit, whose shared epitaph reads: "For half a century missionaries of the gospel to the Chinese people."

A beautiful tombstone featuring the two hands clasped in friendship—or, the land of the dead welcoming the deceased to eternal life—seemed to glow in the light of the hot afternoon.

Mary, died aged 25 yrs, 2 mo, 8 D's, the beloved wife of J.M. Pitts. I loved that Mary, "a native of New York," was the one to greet me to Mountain View. Sadly, at the bottom of her stone was the marker for Lenabelle, perhaps her daughter, who died at "11 yrs, 6 mo.s, 23 Dys."

In the distance I could see an interesting-looking mausoleum with an angel standing guard in front. I walked over, still heading in the direction of Julia Morgan, to take a look. The Twombly mausoleum houses the remains of the founder of Oakland's First National Gold Bank. The angel, standing to the side of the entrance, looks up toward the heavens, holding the Book of Life in one hand and a quill in the other. One wing was cracked down the top but had been repaired. Her beseeching marble face ran down in weathered white streaks against the brown of age, making it appear as though she were crying.

There was an extremely unusual tombstone for Nellie, who died in 1879. At the top there was an engraving of a swan feeding her chicks in the nest. Underneath it, there was a banner that read: "For our young we perish." I did some online research into this symbol and the quotation, but all I found was another cemetery photographer who had stumbled on to this same tombstone years ago and was also a bit creeped out by it.

I had just about given up on finding Julia Morgan, but I figured I had come this far and so I should continue. I walked all the way down a path into the side of the mountain, and back, scanning the tombstones, a trickle of water from the fountain the only sound. Finally, I found the stone. Kristie was right; there wasn't much to write home about. Just the names of the Morgans, with Julia's, 1872–1957, falling in the middle of the list.

Despite her architectural achievements, not much is known about Morgan's personal life. Chapel of the Chimes, one of her major projects, is just adjacent to Mountain View. Despite my desire to celebrate her, the anonymity seemed fitting, as she was, in life, an incredibly private person.

Up the footpath was an unfinished tombstone, for Baby Ramsey, who entered the world and left it the same day, and presumably their mother, Bemmie R., wife of H. Ramsey But neither H. Ramsey nor any other family members were to be found on the rest of the stone. At the top there were oak leaves and what I believe to be ferns, in the process of unraveling, caught in the moment just before. The mausolea of Millionaires' Row are certainly something

to see, but I prefer this strange little stone for Bemmie and Baby Ramsey.

Mountain View was kind enough to permit me to visit a second time. As I made my way into the cemetery, I realized that this was the first time in six months that I had done my fieldwork alone. In the beginning of lockdown even the playgrounds were closed, so my husband and son would usually accompany me on my research trips. Kristie had

made it clear that I was the only one welcome to walk the grounds. I'm accustomed to being one of the few people in a cemetery, but this time I was truly alone. As I walked farther inside, away from the construction at the front, the total quiet and stillness became more apparent. It was eerie.

The public had always been allowed at Mountain View before the lockdown. In a society that stigmatizes our cemeteries and operates under a deep denial of death through the hospitalization of death and the popularity of direct cremation, it doesn't surprise me that hordes of people looking for fresh air have no idea how to comport themselves in a cemetery.

Outside the beautiful and completely empty main mausoleum, I noticed another pyramid tomb, the Gwin mausoleum. William McKendree Gwin was a California pioneer who argued that California should become a state. When it did, he was awarded by becoming its first senator, as his epitaph reads. But Gwin's legacy was complicated. According to Grey Brechin's

Imperial San Francisco, "under cover of the Civil War . . . Gwin, sought the help of the French emperor to 'colonize' the northern states of Mexico with Confederate refugees. . . . The defeat of the Confederacy ended Gwin's hopes for a mining empire of his own. . . . The former senator returned to California after a brief stint in prison at Fort Jackson, Florida, recouping his fortunes in a Sierra gold mine and his status as a leader of San Francisco society. His great-grandson, Gwin Follis, became the president of Standard Oil of California."

Next to the Gwin mausoleum, a much smaller tombstone for a woman named Jane read "the memory of the just is blessed."

Two scary sphinxes guarded the mausoleum at the top of the hill. This is the resting place of David Colton, the legal counsel to the Transcontinental Railroad. When Colton died, his wife had this mausoleum built at the top of the hill in Mountain View so that it would be visible from their Nob Hill mansion in San Francisco. Designed by Fulgenzio Seregeni, the ornate mausoleum reveals another layer of beauty inside, a beautiful portrait of an angel in stained glass, taking off his robe and revealing his wings, in bright, rather patriotic primary colors.

This wasn't Millionaires' Row, but it was a section of notable Bay Area personalities. Just down the path from the Colton mausoleum, I saw a large slab monument for a man named Washington Bartlett, born in Savannah, Georgia, a mayor of San Francisco and governor of California, and apparently the first Jewish man to hold both offices.

Around the corner there was a beautiful line of about seven mausolea built into the hillside. No doubt these were expensive at the time they were constructed. Unlike those on Millionaires' Row, though, they were in poorer condition, mostly from age. Peeking inside, one revealed an ornate Greek mosaic, and another a Byzantine portrait of Christ.

Making my way down the path, out of the corner of my eye I could see a large Elk statue marking the resting place of members of the fraternal order. But just as I took a photo, two actual deer, with antlers appeared at the top of the hill, observing me cautiously. As I stood there among the legal counsel to the Transcontinental Railroad, the Presidents of Standard Oil, the first senators and governors of the state of California, I thought about the people who did the actual labor for these titans of industry: the indigenous people, the Mexican people, Asian immigrants, Black Americans. These people aren't buried at Mountain View, though they most likely also built these gorgeous tombs. Exhumation and desecration if a very real threat to the dead in the Bay Area. The cemetery has to protect its staff, and its permanent residents. It's important to recognize who enjoys that protection.

There was a sweeping path back down the hill, with the rest of Mountain View stretching out toward its borders. I could see St. Mary's on the other side. I came into a shaded area where there were a few very old gravestones to my right, in a section with no remaining footpaths. A small stone fence guarded the space, and in the back, there were fences and gates in all varying condition, revealing homes on the other side. This is the oldest section of the cemetery, or as Mountain View calls it, "the unendowed section." If graves are unendowed, it means they didn't receive funds for upkeep, so the cemetery can do whatever they please with them. Clearly most of these graves were too old to have families to claim them, though perhaps there were newer burials without markers.

It was the week before Thanksgiving, and as I walked up the path to get a better look at this area, I came upon an entire flock of wild turkeys nibbling in the dirt. "Don't make eye contact," I thought to myself. When I walked by, they regarded me impassively, but I needed to get up there and back into this area. As I hopped up the small stone border, one of the turkeys, startled, gobbled and flapped their wings.

There were several Victorian-era tombstones near the back, some in German. One stone for Charles Freeman had sunk down into the earth, but I could still read his epitaph: "Simple — Pure — Steadfast."

There was a more modern ground plaque just next to Charles, for a woman who lived to be nearly 100 with a quotation from poet

Joyce Kilmer: "I think I shall never see a poem lovely as a tree." The simple overgrown beauty of this section was dazzling in the early morning sunlight. A beautiful tombstone bore an inscription from Sister Lill: "Sleep on sweet Bessie, take thy rest. God called thee home he thought it best."

At the end of this section, near the back fence of the cemetery, I could see the backyard of one of the houses with a trampoline and other children's toys. What a view—I could only be jealous. There was an abandoned looking shed and several tombstones laying in front, cracked and stacked on top of one another.

In a group still standing, an incredible tombstone appeared with the symbol of the hand pointing upwards to heaven. "Our home," its inscription read, "it's all bright up there."

There are three reservoirs inside Mountain View, held by a dam that eventually empties into Oakland's Lake Merritt. The cemetery uses these for irrigation and drains them near to empty during the summer when the land in the cemetery is particularly dry. That afternoon at Mountain View the first reservoir was bright green, I'd assume from algae. The tombstones set against a lime-green backdrop looked surreal. The reservoir behind this one was much larger, but didn't hold much water. A lone white egret stood at the bottom, looking for something to eat.

I walked down the bridge path between the two and ended up in a more central section. I could see the fountain down at the bottom of the hill, meaning I was near to the main drive. An imposing, gigantic obelisk bore down on me, the resting place of Washington Ryer, a doctor who insulted another physician, Dr. Langdon, in public, in 1856. Langdon had his cronies beat up Ryer, who responded by challenging him to a duel. The police stopped the duel, but Ryer returned in a secret attack and shot the guy in the knee. He survived but "died a cripple," according to *Mountain View People*, a blog on Mountain View's permanent residents by Michael Culbruno. Dr. Ryer apparently suffered no consequences

as a result of the shooting and was considered a "pillar" of the community, as his grave would reflect.

In my meeting with Kristie, she had mentioned that the cemetery cannot share the location of one grave with curious visitors—that of the Black Dahlia, Elizabeth Short, a young woman whose brutal 1947 murder in Los Angeles remains unsolved. "Obviously, people find it on their own," Kristie said. "There's nothing we can do about that. But the family expressly stated in our agreement that they don't want us to give out its location."

Most have heard the story of the Black Dahlia. Short's death has been the subject of many a true-crime account, a novel by James Ellroy, and adapted for television and the big screen, most notably by Brian De Palma in 2006.

True crime, in particular violence against white women, is a source of endless fascination in the United States. "America loves crime stories because America is a crime story," as the beginning of the film *Fargo* tells us. But heinous crimes committed against women are objects of particular obsession. Our novels, movies, and television shows can attest to our culture's glamorization of "dead girls."

Elizabeth Short was a real person and a young woman just arriving at adulthood when she was violently murdered. She was born in Massachusetts, and her father abandoned the family when she was a young child. His discarded car made everyone believe he had died by suicide although he hadn't. Smart moved to Vallejo, where her father had recently resurfaced, and fell in love with a pilot, but it was World War II, and her fiancé was killed in a plane crash less than a week before the end of the war. His death spurred her move to Los Angeles.

Some say Short had aspirations to be an actress, which is where the "Black Dahlia" name probably comes from—a noir film, *The Blue Dahlia*, had just been released in 1946. Short was a young white woman with jet-black hair.

She lived in Los Angeles just six months before she was murdered. A woman out for a walk with her daughter thought she saw a discarded mannequin on the side of the road. But it was the body of Elizabeth Short, cut in half, posed by her killer. Her mouth was slashed from ear to ear. Smart's murder became the first crime to capture national attention in postwar America. The level of brutality makes it horrifically unforgettable. Though there have been many theories as to the identity of her killer, Elizabeth Short's murder has never been solved.

I had made my way though Mountain View that afternoon with the plan of eventually finding Short's grave. It wasn't difficult, as Kristie had mentioned, to find directions online as to its location. But when I arrived at the fountain, I found myself lost. The directions had said to take the "steps" up to the left of the mausoleum. I did so, and wandered around for several minutes. No Black Dahlia. I felt guilty about perpetuating the sensationalism surrounding of her death. I wandered up and down the hillside, arguing with myself over whether or not to include Elizabeth Short in this chapter, questioning my motives.

There was of course plenty to see aside from Short's small, unassuming ground plaque. But I felt I had come this far, and I knew I could not return to Mountain View without permission. This reaffirmed my desire to find her, and I turned around. My

GPS said I was in the completely wrong location. So I walked back down the very steep hill toward the main road. In doing so I noticed that there were actual steps here. Back toward the mausoleum there weren't steps exactly, it was more of a path. The directions had specified "steps." Perhaps I was in the wrong section. So I walked back to the beginning of the steps and counted out the rows, then walked down the graves. She was there.

Her plaque is pink and black marble, emblazoned with her initials and her name and dates. Her only epitaph is "daughter."

I have often wondered why Short is buried at Mountain View. At the time of her murder, she was living in Los Angeles, and her mother in New York. She had gone to Vallejo to reconnect with her father, but it didn't go so well. They argued, and she moved. Apparently he was not present at her funeral. Research revealed that two of Short's sisters had settled in the Bay Area, one in Berkeley. Perhaps she was familiar with Mountain View. I can only imagine that the family was eager to escape Los Angeles and the insane attention from the media. Short's body was flown down to Oakland and buried here at Mountain View.

When I posted the image I had taken of this grave, it predictably got a big response. What interested me, though, were the ways in which people acted protective of Short. They seemed to want to rewrite her story. Some claimed she was buried at Mountain View because her father lived in Vallejo, and that he had identified the body. I don't think this is true, and it seems to indicate people's hope to posthumously reunite the estranged father and daughter. Kristie had told me it was a privilege for Mountain View to be open to the public, and she's right. But it is also a privilege to be buried at Mountain View. Public interest in Short's murder and the impulse to protect her remains is not a protection that all people receive, in life or in death.

I looked down at Short's plaque. It was, like the other ground plaques on this steep hill, slightly raised, coming out of the brown grass. I looked to her direct left, there was a man named Otto here, and down the line a reverend, and a woman named Zora Monk. Strangers.

The funeral was a lonely one, with only Short's mother, sister, and brother-in-law in attendance. Two men in trench coats, *SF Weekly* reported, either press agents, or, more likely, plainclothes policemen, watched from the fountain.

After the burial, Short's mother moved to Oakland. She wanted to be closer to her surviving daughters in the Bay Area, and closer to Short, here at Mountain View. She returned to the East Coast in the 1970s. In explaining her choice to bury her daughter here at Mountain View, Short's mother told reporters in 1947, "she's buried here because she loved California."

EXCLUSIVE USE

As most of my time at Mountain View had been spent in the older part of the cemetery, I hadn't come across many portraits. But as I stopped to take a photo of a beautiful tree, I noticed someone smiling at me from a plaque in the ground:

Aramis
Matthews
Fouché
1904–2001

Owner of Fouché's Hudson Funeral Home, a gentleman, a self-made man, a proud man, a man of vision, businessman, mentor, entrepreneur, philanthropist, community activist, civil rights pioneer.

Mr. Fouché wasn't smiling, exactly, but gazing confidently, chin raised, in a suit and tie. From his obituary in the *East Bay Times*: "As a Civil Rights Leader, his lobby at the nation's capital initiated the erasure of the 'Whites Only' clause on land deeds in California. The resulting effect on the Black community from these endeavors was economic power and freedom to purchase land in previously restricted areas. Many business and churches attribute their existence to Mr. Fouché."

Black-owned businesses like Fouché's Hudson Funeral Home are integral to their communities. But most were are created out of a need for services denied to that community by virulent racism. The National Funeral Directors Association began as a Black Funeral Directors Association. According to Angelika Krüger-Kahloula, who writes in her crucial article "On the Wrong Side of the Fence: Racial Segregation in American Cemeteries," the National Funeral Directors Association "started as the Independent National Negro Funeral Directors Association in 1925. The name underwent a series of changes, from the Progressive Funeral Directors Association a few years after its founding, to the National Negro Funeral Directors Association in 1938, and to National Negro Funeral Directors and Morticians Association in 1957, before the racial tag was dropped."

Racism is a necessary consideration in writing about American cemeteries given that, as Krüger-Kahloula's research finds, "until the 1950s, about 90 percent of all public cemeteries in the U.S. employed a variety of racial restrictions."

Some of the examples are particularly heinous, like that of Army Specialist 4 Pondexteur E. Williams. When he was killed in action in Vietnam in 1970, his mother wanted to bury him at Hillcrest Cemetery in Fort Pierce, Florida. He was turned away. "A white acquaintance of the family had donated a gravesite, next to that of her infant grandson," Krüger-Kahloula relates, "but was forbidden to let the Williamses use it." His mother told the *New York Times*, "I feel that he being black and can't be buried in Hillcrest, then he didn't have any business going to the war. He died for nothing."

Standing at the foot of Mr. Fouché's grave at Mountain View, I wondered whether Mountain View had ever included racist restrictions in their cemetery.

In *Long vs. Mountain View*, in 1955, Clara Mae Long wanted to put her husband's remains in a mausoleum at Mountain View "set aside for the exclusive use for members of the Caucasian race." In denying Long's appeal, the California District Court of Appeal cited a similar case, Rice vs. Sioux City Memorial Park, which had upheld that places of "public accommodation" must provide equal access to all races, places like "restaurants" . . . but that cemeteries were not included in this list.

Fascinatingly, the presiding justice, a man named Nourse, added a caveat to his decision: "I cannot resist a word of protest. I cannot believe that a man's mortal remains will disintegrate any less peaceably because of the close proximity of the body of a member of another race, and in that inevitable disintegration I am sure that the pigmentation of the skin cannot long endure. It strikes me that the carrying of racial discrimination into the burial grounds is a particularly stupid form of human arrogance and intolerance. If life does not do so, the universal fellowship of death should teach humility. The good people who insist on the racial segregation of what is mortal in man may be shocked to learn when their own lives end that God has reserved no racially exclusive position for them in the hereafter."

Writing about American history is often deeply depressing in its expansiveness of imperial racism and misogyny. Justice Nourse's words are undoubtedly moving, but a judgment in favor of Mrs. Long would have been much more effective.

Mr. Fouré was a pillar of his community, and it makes sense that he is buried at Mountain View, one of the most famous cemeteries in the United States and certainly in California, along-side many prominent men and women who shaped the Bay Area and made notable differences in the way Oakland and Bay Area residents live even today. His presence at Mountain View, amidst the realities of this racist past, illustrates why it is so important to study our cemeteries, to confront these truths and to acknowledge systemic racism in our history and culture.

"Cemetery desegregation was only to be achieved via the Supreme Court's 1968 Jones v. Mayer decision, which actually referred back to an 1866 civil rights law," Krüger-Kahloula writes. "The original provision guaranteed blacks equal rights in making and enforcing contracts and purchasing personal property."

Returning to Oakland, the place of her birth, Gertrude Stein wrote, "There is no there there." She didn't mean it as a negative comment, necessarily, but rather that everything had changed.

I knew very little about Oakland when I moved to the Bay Area, aside from a vague idea that it was a Black community being rapidly gentrified. We passed by the BART Fruitvale station and my mind immediately went to the murder of Oscar Grant, an unarmed man who was shot in the back as a police officer pinned him to the ground with his knee on New Year's Day in 2009 in Fruitvale Station. Grant died at the hospital later that day, and the policeman was charged with involuntary manslaughter.

We moved to the East Bay on February 1. Ahmaud Arbery was murdered on February 23. Breonna Taylor was murdered on March 13. George Floyd was murdered on May 25. Angela Davis spoke from the sunroof of a car at one of the protests, surrounded by masked protestors.

Oakland is the birthplace of the Black Panthers, founded in 1966 by Merritt College students Huey Newton and Bobby Seale. At the time of the party's founding, despite Oakland's large Black population, only 16 out of 661 Oakland police officers were Black. Police brutality and violence against Black people in Oakland was rampant.

The Black population in Oakland skyrocketed during what is known as the Second Gold Rush. During World War II, the Bay Area became a place of major defense work, and Oakland's port remains the busiest in the Bay Area. Black Americans and other minority groups flooded the region looking for sustainable work. "Between 1940 and 1945 the black population of the Bay Area grew from 19,759 to 64,680, or by more than 27 percent," Marilynn Johnson writes in *The Second Gold Rush: Oakland and the East Bay in World War II*. "The defense mobilization of WWII permanently transformed the West Coast urban economy . . . . increased racial and regional diversity would remain a permanent feature of urban life, long outliving the economic forces that brought it about."

Mountain View wasn't the only cemetery to practice these racist restrictions in the Bay Area. "White businesspeople responded to the black influx by attempting to codify segregation measures for public establishments," Johnson points out. "Even in death, black residents were segregated. Contra-Costa's Sunset Cemetery, an integrated burial ground in the prewar era, closed its gates to black residents during World War II."

The racial provisions in cemeteries reflected racial covenants in real estate. In the decade following World War II, the defense workers had that come to work in the Bay Area and returning BIPOC veterans found themselves discriminated against when it came to renting or purchasing a home. As San Francisco rapidly expanded, a housing shortage pushed minority groups out of the city and into the East Bay.

"When Richmond razed hundreds of acres of war housing to open up land for private development . . . the city evicted thousands of minority and low-income tenants," Johnson writes, "sowing the seeds of racial discontent that would plague Richmond and other East Bay cities for decades." It was the climate of racism out of which the Black Panthers were born. It is the same racial violence we suffer from today.

Mountain View is part of Oakland, but there are many different Oaklands. The largest city in Alameda County, there are fifty distinct neighborhoods in Oakland. Piedmont is its own independent city, "entirely surrounded by Oakland." It is entirely surrounded by Oakland because it is *in* Oakland. In 1907 the "city" refused to be annexed by Oakland and sought its own incorporation. As a result it has its own police force, school system, and government. As of 2010, according to the census, Piedmont was 74.2 percent white.

In addition to St. Mary's, the Catholic cemetery just adjacent to Mountain View, there is another cemetery that calls Oakland Home, Evergreen Cemetery, located in the Eastmont neighborhood. When I typed "Eastmont, Oakland" into Google, the first return was "is Eastmont Oakland safe?"

Evergreen Cemetery, and the neighborhood in which it rests, is just a twelve-minute drive from the gates of Mountain View. But the cemeteries could not be more different.

After a few hot weeks, the weekend we visited Evergreen was refreshingly cool, almost like a real autumn day. Just before we reached the entrance gates we passed a Little League game on the right side of the street. We pulled into the cemetery, which was cut in half by Camden Street, and parked up the hill from the office.

The cemetery was much larger than I expected, with hundreds of tombstones across a long, sloping hill. I could tell immediately that many were old, and had sunken into the ground, giving the landscape an eerie, crooked vista. The only stones that stood upright and straight in any uniform structure were the military tablets that belonged to the veterans' section.

In addition to the many tombstones, there were also many flat memorial plaques in the ground. I try to steer as best I can away from walking directly on top of graves, but in Evergreen, this was impossible.

It had been foggy when we first arrived. My husband and son went one way, playing with a large palm frond, and I went the other. The sun broke through the clouds. The light was unbelievable.

There was the grave of a young girl who died in 1976 at just seventeen. Behind her, a Black husband and wife, he dressed in his army uniform, smiled up at me.

A beautiful tombstone with the epitaphs of Mom, Dad, and their son encased in hearts popped out of the green-brown grass. I looked down and noticed there was a military plaque in the ground, and did a quick search. The son was killed in action in Vietnam. He was twenty. A website that commemorates those whose names are included on the wall of the Vietnam Veterans Memorial in Washington, DC, features two photos of this young man. In one, he stands shirtless, rifle across his shoulders, behind a wall of sandbags, his combat boots dusty. Smiling, he wears his dog tag and I can just make out tattoos on his chest and arms.

As I made my way through the long sloping hill, more of the cemetery opened up. Nearly every patch of land was covered in tombstones, some jumbled together, matching in material and color. One granite tombstone for "Professor F. Hamilton" featured the unusual design of what looked like a parachute and a deflating hot air balloon. Just behind him, I took in a lovely pinkish granite tombstone adorned with pine cones for two men with different last names. Later, an Instagram follower found that they were father and son in-law.

Without really planning, I was making my way to the large white structure at the top of the hill. I assumed it was a mausoleum.

The white building was now clearly visible. As I stopped to take a photo, it was now impossible to ignore that the side of the building was completely warped, almost as if it had been on fire at some point. Upon closer inspection, I noticed there were several smokestacks attached to the back of the building, which was covered in a mesh fence where several white vans were parked.

Still blissfully ignorant, I approached the building, looking at its beautiful bronze doors and hoping they might be open. There was a strange granite plaque just next to the door, with a long list of names and no other information. I went back to the side of the building that looked burned. One window had been completely blown out, and a piece of wood covered in some kind of tarp had been a makeshift replacement. But the heat source was obviously still present, as the covering itself had warped and bubbled up, exposing the wood.

It was not until I walked around to the other side of the building, hoping for an entrance, that I realized what was going on. We

were completely alone in the cemetery aside from a few trucks that had driven up and parked, their drivers disappearing into the building. This was a crematorium. It was on. Men were working there.

There were several large trucks parked behind the building that I now realized were used for the transportation of bodies. The large white building did look like a mausoleum, and I would wager to guess that it was—but at some point the cemetery added the crematory to the back of the building and closed it off to the public. Maybe they even moved the occupants of the mausoleum someplace else. Perhaps those were the names on that granite plaque.

I ran up the stairs to try the bronze door just in case. It was locked. Just beside the entrance was a pile of clothes, boxes, and food containers. I made a hasty retreat back down the stairs.

One of the major monuments at Evergreen is the Jonestown Memorial to the victims of the Jonestown massacre, in which 918 people died on November 18, 1978, in Jonestown, Guyana. They were members of a cult called the People's Temple led by Jim Jones. I had bypassed the Jonestown Memorial on my way to figure out what I was seeing, so I doubled back to it, located in a small section of grass and trees behind the crematorium. Just adjacent to it on the left was the "scattering garden," a small section with small plaques for cremains.

Underneath a large tree on the very edge of the cemetery gates is one stand-alone tombstone, bookended by benches. It reads: "In memory of the victims of the Jonestown Tragedy Nov. 18, 1978 Jonestown, Guyana, Guyana Emergency Relief Committee." In front of the stone there is a large reddish panel that contains four large tablets of names. In the front of those panels, there is a small stone with a place for flowers that reads: "Jonestown Memorial, These plaques were dedicated May 29, 2011, More than 150 relatives and friends contributed to their creation and installation with sincere appreciation to Evergreen Cemetery. Rest in Peace."

2011 seems like an awfully long time to wait to construct a memorial. Wondering why the Jonestown Memorial is here at

Evergreen is easily explained: 412 of the bodies of the deceased were unclaimed and taken in by Evergreen and buried in this exact spot in a mass grave, so plans for a memorial here for the victims felt natural. However, the plans came to a screeching halt when the parties involved, including the families of those who died, argued over whether or not Jim Jones, the cult leader responsible for their deaths, should be included. Most were more than comfortable leaving his name off the memorial. But others, including Jones's son, fought for him to be included. After thirty-two years of legal battles, a judge finally ruled, and his name, "James Warren Jones" does appear here.

The Jonestown Massacre occurred in Guyana, but many of the victims were from the Bay Area. "To this day it's difficult to find one local resident over the age of 30 who doesn't have ties to at least one of the 918 victims," according to *Atlas Obscura*. "The motive for refusing to omit the name of the man responsible for such a tragic loss of life was to preserve historical record and include the names of everyone who died that day, even Jones, who is listed in alphabetical order with no special attention or disclaimer—just one more name in a sea of loss." Eighty percent of the members of the People's Temple were Black. In photographs of the carnage of that day, there are so many bodies. The vast majority of them are Black bodies.

The combination of mass murder-suicide against the backdrop of an operational crematory had me wondering where my family had wandered off to. I could hear my son crying in the distance. Just after I passed a sign that said "Danger: Old Trees," they appeared at the top of the hill. My son was crying out, "I want you!" I picked him up and asked my husband if they'd seen the Jonestown Memorial. "We saw it," he acknowledged, "but I'm not sure I remember what Jonestown is." "Do you know the expression 'drink the Kool-Aid?'" I asked him. As soon as the words "Kool-Aid" came out of my mouth his face changed.

We walked back down the hill, passing a tombstone with a marker stuck into the ground that looked like it had been decorated by schoolchildren. "Mom: the heart of the family," it read. There were several pinwheels on the graves near where we'd parked. I reminded my son he could look but not touch. I took a few photographs of a mausoleum then we walked to the back. I was eager to get to the rest of the cemetery, but he had other ideas. He wanted to see more pinwheels.

"Look, Mama," he said, "eggplants!" Fairly certain he had seen some kind of flower or berry and mistaken it for eggplants, I walked over to where he was standing. But there was a pile of long, thin eggplants behind the mausoleum, and a sweatshirt strewn across the grass. Looking closely, I noticed about ten or so pennies next to the eggplants in the dirt. "Can I hold them?" he asked. "Can I hold them . . . in my hands?"

It's not uncommon to see fruit, water, paper money or other small gifts in cemeteries, as Chinese tradition calls for these offerings to be made to the dead. But these eggplants were hidden behind the mausoleum. There were no Chinese graves nearby. And the Chinese burn paper money, not pennies. As I steered my child away from the suspicious eggplants, I made sure to photograph the scene for further research.

When I searched the mysterious "eggplants and cemeteries," though, I got lots of hits. Eggplants and pennies are an offering to Oya, a protector of cemeteries and the dead. Oya is an orisha, or a spirit, that hails from the religion of the Yoruba in present day Nigeria. Other forms of orisha are present in Voodoo practice and Santería. Oya loves eggplants, dark chocolate, and she keeps a strict accounting of her favors, hence, the pennies.

It is still extremely rare to see these kind of offerings in a cemetery, anywhere. "'Gentrification,' that is, 'cleaning up' the graveyard," Kübler-Kohloula writes, "usually entails the removal of folk decorations and plants that might obstruct the run of the electric lawn mower."

Just down the path, there was a large monument with a bas-relief carving of an exhausted soldier, spear in hand, atop his equally downtrodden horse. This tableau is a copy of a famous 1915 sculpture by James Earle Fraser called *The End of the Trail*, which depicts a tired Native American man atop his horse. Fraser said he was inspired to create the statue based on his time as a child in Dakota Territory, where a trapper once said to him "the Indians will someday be pushed into the Pacific Ocean." Though the statue recognizes the genocide committed against the Native people of this country, in the early 1900s, it was a popular theme for tombstones and monuments, symbolizing the end of life.

By this time, my son had had enough and went back to the car with his dad to wait for me to finish up. I walked down what I initially thought was a footpath, only to discover that the entire space was filled in with graves, no standing tombstones, but ground plaques. These were much more recent in comparison to the stones on the hill, so one could assume this had been a path but out of necessity the cemetery had to put it use.

Many of the plaques bore photo portraits, including an adorable smiling young couple, "together forever." At the end of this path, I seemed to be transitioning back into the past again, with graves in the early 1900s. Some were written in Italian. One obelisk listed its occupant as a "native of Azores." A young woman named Martha, her tombstone marked by a wilting rose, died in 1888, fourteen years before this cemetery was established.

A gigantic tree stump looked like a natural monument, but then I noticed there was in fact a bronze plaque at its base, with two concrete blocks on either side. What monument had been here, and how had it been incorporated into this tree, obviously older than the cemetery and probably Oakland itself?

Freemasons, Woodmen of the World, natives of Germany, babies, Catholics, were all jumbled together here, as if the ground itself was moving, tombstones wobbled and leaned in every direction. Two, marked Papa and Mama, had completely sunken into

the ground, only the tops sticking out of the ground, enough for me to see the Odd Fellows' symbol, the three-link chain, on Papa's. So perhaps these older graves, the ones that predate the cemetery, were moved from Odd Fellows in San Francisco.

A little girl's grave was marked with one fake pink flower, though she died, just twelve, in 1934. "Our darling," I could barely read, "God knew best."

I could have easily spent several more hours here, taking in each and every section with all their secrets, but I felt pulled to the front of the cemetery—well, at least what used to be its front gates—where a patch of about a dozen uniform large black tombstones piqued my curiosity.

As I rounded the corner to see the front of these graves, a crow squawked at me from the original cemetery gates, locked up and closed for who knows how long. A man in a house across the street was washing his car and singing along to the radio.

The script was very clear once I came around the corner. HELLS ANGELS, each one read, with the flaming skull logo, MC OAKLAND. I'd never seen one Hells Angels gravestone, much less twelve, all together. Each stone was emblazoned with the man's name, his nickname, dates, and portrait. Two of them, on the reverse side, featured the names of their wives or girlfriends, a common practice on military tombstones.

It's difficult to grapple with the presence of the Hells Angels at Evergreen. The group has a history of virulent racism, misogyny, racial violence, and ties to white supremacist groups. In 1969, a Black eighteen-year-old named Meredith Hunter was beaten and stabbed to death by Hells Angel Alan Passaro at a Rolling Stones concert in Altamont, California. Passaro was acquitted on grounds of self-defense. As recently as last year, a Hells Angel was arrested after vandalizing an auto parts store in Minneapolis during the protests on the murder of George Floyd. According to the affidavit, the man wanted to "sow discord and racial unrest."

One could not imagine this violent group would be welcomed at most cemeteries. At Evergreen, the dissonance is palpable. To the right, there is an elegant stone for a young Black man named Prymus, "resting" since 1933.

A completely empty receiving vault stood in the distance, near the street, its metal doors locked for years. I peered in, there was nothing but cobwebs and empty crypts.

As I made my way back to the car, I went into my usual panic mode, snapping photographs willy-nilly, trying to capture as much as possible for my notes. One stately tombstone with bright yellow flowers stood against the hillside. I took a photo purely for its physical beauty. In the car, on the way back home, I swiped through my photos from the day. I stopped at this one to take a closer look. It was the resting place of three people: Husband, wife, and their son, who had died at just three years old. Above his name was a white dove. But then I saw that the mother and father had the same date of death, just four days after their son.

I searched their names in newspaper records. George and Diane Mendenhall had tried for eight years to have a baby. When they finally became parents, in 1981, to Joshua, they were overjoyed. But tragically, on Father's Day in 1984, Joshua wandered into a small pond behind their house, fell, and drowned. He remained in a coma for five days before George and Diane made the excruciating decision to take him off life support on June 21, 1984.

At some point, after his death, Joshua's parents made the decision to take their own lives. They mailed two letters, one to their neighborhood babysitting group, warning them of "death traps" and urging them to look out for the risks to their children's safety. The other letter was to the funeral home handling Joshua's arrangements, Sorensen Brothers Mortuary, informing them that they should expect a "triple funeral." As soon as the funeral home received the letter they called the police, but, as a representative told the Associated Press, "unfortunately, we were too late."

Evergreen was founded in 1903, and it is full, but still operates the crematorium for direct cremation through the Nautilus Society. Reading through the Yelp page, the reviews are not good. Family members are distraught over the condition of the grounds despite the fact that the cemetery is one of endowment care. According to these reviews, their complaints have been met with a lack of a response by the cemetery's office, and as a last resort, many have filed official reports with the Cemetery Department Board of Consumer Affairs.

In reading these complaints, I'm reminded that while I might see unkempt grounds as charming, even beautiful, the family members of the deceased are entitled to be outraged by a lack of care, especially if, in their fees for burial, the cemetery includes endowment care, or perpetual care. I hope Alameda County will give the attention to these problems that they so obviously deserve. Evergreen is not a Black cemetery, but it is in a Black neighborhood, and many of the people buried here are Black.

The very first grave I spied when I got out of the car at Evergreen was that of Earl "Fatha" Hines, a jazz pianist." Dizzy Gillespie and Charlie Parker were both members of his band. Hines played a show just before he died of a heart attack in 1984. He was a giant of jazz.

"The graveyard, *locus mémoriae* in the literal sense, provides the members of a given community with geographic and historical roots. It is a place to return to, in life or in death," Kübler-Kohloula writes. Roots are not easily accessible for many Black Americans, due to the erasure of their family history in the genocide of American slavery. The funeral home owned by Aramis Fouché was not only a community service, it was a way of establishing roots. Cemeteries are one way of tapping into our past. Recognizing that BIPOC Americans are subject to discrimination even in death and taking the steps to honor their burial places is essential in the fight against systemic racism—to ensure that Black Lives Matter.

PART IV

WHAT REMAINS

THE GUTTER

"Excuse me," a man said, standing about ten feet away with his family, "but, do you mind my asking what you are photographing?"

We were in Buena Vista Park, in San Francisco's Laurel Heights. He and his family were standing nearby on the path. The adults were socially distancing, standing six feet apart and wearing masks, but their children played together, no masks.

"These are tombstones," I said, as casually as I could.

"What," he replied, as if he had misheard me.

"Tombstones," I said, "here, in the gutter." I moved aside so he could take a step up, and look. "If you look here, you can see this one says, 'Died,' and you can almost make out the date."

"Oh," he said, with a horrified look on his face, ". . . my God!"

I explained that they were scattered and broken up all up and down the gutters of this section of the path.

Since I decided to write about the cemeteries of San Francisco and the Bay Area I had known I wanted to make it to Buena Vista Park. On a beautiful day we made our way up the huge hills of the city, and parked just in front of the steps to the entrance. Its paths go even higher, leading to a grassy vista at its peak. My son did not want to walk, and frankly I could not blame him.

On our way up to the top, I only saw one broken stone, "E" the only visible letter. I had been led to believe through research that there were many of tombstones, near the playground. Where was the playground? We seemed to be walking up and up. I stopped a group of college age people and asked about the playground. (It seemed ill-advised to ask "where are the tombstones?") They responded that it was on completely the other side of the hill. So we kept walking.

At the peak there was a nice place to sit down and a couple with a large dog that my son seemed interested in. I offered to go on ahead down the other side of the hill, sensing that my husband needed to take a break. I made my way down the other side of the hill, my eyes scanning the gutters as I walked. No tombstones.

I seemed to walk forever, but it always seems longer when you don't know where you're going. Buena Vista Park was gorgeous, with huge trees and wonderful colors. It wasn't hot quite yet, though, as usual, I was overdressed.

Finally, some stones started to appear, like leaves running down a babbling brook. I could just make out Hebrew letters on the first one, and the number 9. A few feet later, a large L. Finally, the stone that clearly read "Died." After a few minutes, the man

approached to ask me what I was doing. The photographs were just so naturally beautiful, set against the other stone of the gutter and surrounding path, scattered with leaves.

I alerted my husband that I had found the stones, and they should make their way down. It took them several minutes but eventually they found me, and eventually, we saw the aforementioned playground in the distance. Like most toddlers, my son loves play-grounds, but in the Bay Area, because of Covid-19, many have been closed. We were wary of having him play on the playground because we were still concerned with surface transmission. At one time, we had been wiping down our groceries and doorknobs.

"Look, Mama!" my son yelled, "a playground!"

I was busy photographing a stone that said, "in memory of L.D. Ebessn," maybe. I tried to explain to my son that the playground was unfortunately closed. His patience tried, he proceeded to have a meltdown, refusing to continue down the path. I calmly explained to my husband that I needed to work and that he'd have to deal with this. As I moved on, I watched as they approached the playground, my husband pointing out the caution tape and bulky chains on the playground's gate.

There were more phantom letters and numbers. "52," "..ny," the word "friends." Names, like "Ann." All in shards and broken pieces.

After San Francisco had evicted cemeteries from the city, beginning in 1914, the relocation left many tombstones unclaimed. Buena Vista Park was opened around 1900, and its popularity

called for more paths and storm drains to be installed, most likely by the WPA in the 1930s. These are pioneer stones are likely from other cemeteries whose age prevented them from having any remaining protectors from demolition.

John W. Blackett of the essential resource website San Francisco Cemeteries writes, "I believe the initial intent was to hide

the original source of these wonderful marble building fragments."
This could be consistent with what I saw at Buena Vista. Most of
the gutters' fragments are facing down, so the text cannot be seen.
But, Blackett writes, "mistakes were made."

Tombstones can also be seen at Ocean Beach and around the
city, especially in places that were once landfills or in repairs made

to sidewalks and gutters after earthquake damage. Many locals of San Francisco have come to believe that the broken tombstones were an effect of the devastating 1906 earthquake, which did indeed damage many cemeteries. But the truth is, the relocation efforts were already underway, especially for older cemeteries outside the Big Four, in the city. Though some were damaged by the earthquake and recycled in this way, most were ground up or smashed by the city when they were left unclaimed by 1930.

I continued to capture a glimpse of letters and numbers in the gutters. One rather large piece clearly read "died, 22nd, 18—, aged 52 years." There were several pieces with no letters or numbers but were obviously parts of tombstones, given the shape and design.

The park wasn't crowded, but there were a few people out for a walk with their dogs or for a jog. No one but yours truly seemed to be interested in the gutters at all. A few people eyed me suspiciously as I set up shots. A particularly beautiful one, laid with colorful red and brown leaves, read "and Feli—" Felix, maybe? "59 yrs."

It was getting to be about that time to head back to the East Bay. I could see my husband, who had given up on getting my son to walk, carrying him toward me down the path.

As I scanned quickly the remaining path, a young, masked couple walked by and the man asked, "sorry, but what are you doing?" I explained like I had to the other man that there were tombstones in the gutters and I was photographing them. "Oh," he said, smiling. "Those are all over the city. You see them everywhere. It's because of the earthquake." His girlfriend turned her head to look at him with a look of surprise. I nodded, internally shaking my head. Satisfied, they continued down the path.

GARDEN OF INNOCENCE

Ericka Karner had been in the midst of a garage renovation at her home in San Francisco's Richmond district in 2016 when her crew hit something solid. It turned out to be a small bronze and lead coffin, 3½ feet long. As the dirt was cleared from the top, two windows emerged, revealing the body of a little girl with long blonde hair, wearing a white dress and holding a rose.

Knowing the history of San Francisco's cemeteries, Karner said the discovery didn't surprise her. But, she told the *Los Angeles Times*, "being a mom, that's unfathomable and sad that a little child could be left behind like that."

Not sure of what to do, Karner called the city, but because the coffin had been found on her property, it was her responsibility. They put Karner in touch with an organization called Garden of Innocence, which raises funds for the reburial of abandoned children. At the time of the discovery, the identity of the little girl was unknown.

Based on the location of Karner's garage, it was most likely that the little girl had been buried in Odd Fellows Cemetery. Researchers were able to narrow down two families to which she could've belonged based on an old map of the cemetery's plots. Taking a few strands from her hair, they tracked down a descendant from one of these families and compared her DNA with his. They got a match, and were able to identify the little girl as Edith Howard Cook.

Edith was born in San Francisco on November 28, 1873. She died just shy of three years later, on October 13, 1876. The cause was marasmus, or "severe undernourishment," scientists deduced, probably caused from a bacterial or viral infection. When her parents buried her, they surrounded her body with eucalyptus leaves, put lavender springs in her hair, and a rosary on top of her chest.

After the DNA had been collected, Edith was buried under a tombstone at Greenlawn Cemetery in Colma with the name "Miranda Eve," a name Karner's daughters had given her, with the

epitaph: "The child loved around the world / If no one grieves, no one will remember." With her identity now known, a new stone marks Edith's grave, with a photo of her resting in her coffin.

> *Edith Howard Cook*
> *Nov. 28, 1873 – Oct. 13, 1876*
> *2 years, 10 months, 15 days old*
> *'I once was lost, but now I'm found'*
> *THANK YOU TEAM MIRANDA!*
> *MIRANDA EVE WAS LAID TO REST*
> *JUNE 4, 2016 (GOOGLE HER) FOR OUR STORY*

When Odd Fellows Cemetery was evicted from San Francisco, its occupants were moved to Greenlawn Cemetery, in Colma. They were all buried in a mass grave, under a single broken obelisk, at the back of Greenlawn's property. You can see the marker for 26,000 graves, potentially including those of Edith's family, from the parking lot of the Colma Home Depot. But the trustees of Odd Fellows left no provision for those people. Legal troubles ensued. "Eventually an embarrassment to Greenlawn," Svanevik and Burgett write in *City of Souls*, "a fence was built around the Odd Fellows memorial and it was cut off from the cemetery." When I visited Greenlawn, Danae showed me the Odd Fellows section. There is an enormous unpaved patch of land that Greenlawn mostly uses for storage of machinery, their dumpster, discarded wreaths, and such. Home Depot loomed large across the way over red sand. A man on a tractor passed by, waving. Over to my right, there was an outcropping of a small farm with people at work watering orange flowers and other plants.

Near the border of the makeshift field there was the Odd Fellows monument. It was a huge obelisk, standing alone in the center of the orange-red dust. The point of the obelisk had broken off at the very tip. As I took a shot of the monument, I noticed there was a Burger King sign in the distance.

Edith is buried at the front of the cemetery. The probability of her family making it to Greenlawn is low, but if they are there, they are still separated by a distance of a few hundred yards.

The organization which helped to connect Edith with the researchers at UC Santa Cruz who were able to identify her, Garden of Innocence, made her funeral at Greenlawn into an event. Most of the people who worked on the "Miranda Eve" team did so pro bono. Ed Green, a professor at UC Santa Cruz, told the *Los Angeles Times*, "People wanted to solve this. It was infectious." Elissa Davey, of Garden of Innocence, encouraged the community to come to Edith's reburial and to bring rose petals to scatter at her final resting place.

The day I went to find Edith Cook was an ominous one. Air quality in the Bay Area was in the toxic zone, as wildfires in wine country still raged. When I pulled into the cemetery, there were two women making an offering near where I thought Edith was located.

In order to give them privacy, I took a stroll around the rest of the cemetery. "It smells like smoke," my husband said, "do you think it's safe for us to be out here?" I told him I thought it was just the smoke from the offering.

My family got in the car, ready to go, as I struggled to locate Edith. The women were long gone. Finally, I found her—her stone was just two down from where they had been burning the paper money. I took a few photographs of Edith's marker, and marveled at her image. She had been in that perfectly sealed coffin for 145 years. I can't imagine what happened when they opened it and she was exposed to oxygen. I looked in the direction of the Odd Fellows obelisk and mass grave.

Toward the tombstone where the women had been, there was the pail for burning, and their offerings—they had left water and oranges for their loved one. But upon closer inspection, there was no burnt money in the bright red metal container. I walked back briskly to car, telling my husband to roll up the windows. "That's not an offering," I said. "It's the fires."

Just after Edith was identified, three more people from Odd Fellows were found in the Richmond neighborhood, left behind. In San Francisco, and all over the Bay Area, burials are constantly unearthed due to development. The frequency of these discoveries in the city comes from the fact that the task of moving the bodies out to Colma was not complete by any means. But it's not just cemetery burials like Edith that are unearthed. There are indigenous burials, the remains thousands of years old, uncovered by the rapid expansion of San Francisco and the Bay Area in the postwar period, up to the current day.

Even in the 1850s, burials were constantly being unearthed. "The 49'ers generally buried their dead in open land nearest to where a man had died. Sometimes it was in the backyard of his house, or it might be in the sand dunes behind his tent," Charles Lockwood writes in *Suddenly San Francisco*. "The city fathers were too busy with the problems of the living to worry about the dead. They did not bother to keep any records of deaths, and there were no municipal inquests into the causes."

In 2014, the skeleton of a young man who lived about 7,500 years ago was unearthed during the construction of the Transbay project in downtown San Francisco. Peter W. Colby, a writer for *Anthropology Now* wanted to get more information on the remains and what the developers planned on doing with the remains. He called the office, and spoke to the receptionist, who "acknowledged to me that Native American remains were found, but 'we don't talk much about them, out of respect for the dead.'" To this day, no one knows for sure whether or not the Transbay man was moved and reburied nearby or in a cemetery, or if he remains there.

The discovery of indigenous burials have proved a complex problem for real estate developers. "Under state law, whenever Native American remains are discovered, the local coroner must notify the California Native American Heritage Commission, which then dispatches a Native American from a list of Most

Likely Descendants," writes Ron Russell at *SF Weekly*. The MLD is supposed to oversee the reburial or removal of the remains on behalf of the tribe. But, as Russell points out in his article, "the law gives MLDs little real power; they can't legally force anyone to comply with their regulations."

There were once 452 shell mounds, or indigenous burial grounds, in the Bay Area. Only three "survive." In Berkeley, a development project was embroiled in legal proceedings since it was announced. The 1900 Fourth Project hoped to build a five-story building with housing, retail, and a parking garage in Berkeley. The Ohlone people claim the site is a shell mound, a sacred burial place. Local historian Richard Schwartz estimates there may be many more, citing the fact that over the decades as Berkeley was developed, 455 human burials have been found within a one-block radius of the proposed 1900 Fourth Project site. The discovery of five human burials on Fourth Street near Spengers Fish Grotto seems to back up the belief that there could be more human remains and artifacts at the site.

"In many ways, the West Berkeley Shellmound is a cautionary tale that teaches the pain a people can experience when they are confronted with the loss of their connection to history, and in particular, their sacred sites," Katherine Malone-France, chief preservation officer for the National Trust for Historic Preservation, told the *Earth Island Journal*. As usual, developers cite the need for housing as reason for the land to be developed, the needs of the living taking precedence over the dead. "Ohlone people are not against the development for affordable housing in our homelands, especially in this time of great need," Corrina Gould, Ohlone leader and spokesperson told *Berkeleyside*, "but this is the very first site of our ancestors along the Bay, and it needs to be protected—for Ohlone people and everyone that lives on this land." The Ohlone propose that the site be developed as a monument and protected by the government. As of April 2021, a California court of appeals has ruled that development of the 1900 project can continue.

The difference between the way these unearthed burials are handled in San Francisco depends on who is being uncovered. Many indigenous burials and artifacts have gone into the University of California system for research. The use of the remains for study is also a point of contention. "Defending his tribe's refusal to allow study of their ancestors' remains, a Bay Area tribal chair asked the *San Francisco Chronicle*: 'How would Jewish or Christian people feel if we wanted to dig up skeletal remains in a cemetery and study them?'" Others have been reburied nearby, and some have remained where they lay, underneath gigantic skyscrapers and transit hubs.

A man named Andrew Galvan, who traces his lineage to the Ohlone people, often acts as a MLD for these development projects. He and his father were deeded a small cemetery in Fremont, California, called the "Ohlone Cemetery," from the Diocese of Oakland, next to Interstate 680, the resting place of approximately 11,000 Ohlone people. Since 1971, Galvan and his father have

managed the reburial of 5,000 native remains from development projects in San Francisco, many of them moved to this cemetery. As Galvan charges a consultation fee and fees for the removal and the cleaning of the remains, his business has drawn concern from the Ohlone. Though he claims his work is not for profit, the Ohlone and preservationists suspect this is not the truth. "There will be a day of reckoning about what's going on down there," tribal chair Rosemary Cambra (who also happens to be Galvan's cousin) told *SF Weekly* in 2007, "and I think Andy knows it."

The contention over the Berkeley Shellmound is just a continuation of the Bay Area's destruction of its cemeteries to make way for development and progress. Yerba Buena Cemetery was closed in 1854, the same year that Lone Mountain (later called Laurel Hill) opened. But the 3,000 bodies there weren't moved to Golden Gate Cemetery until 1870. According to Charles Lockwood, the process was done "so carelessly," with many remains and monuments being lost. But there's a difference between the way in which indigenous burials are dealt with and the extreme sensitivity that was undertaken on behalf of little Edith Cook. The difference is, Edith was white.

We live in the East Bay Hills, an area particularly vulnerable to wildfires. When we're under a red flag warning, we have to be ready to evacuate our home at any time. That means packing a go bag with everything we need, and taking essential documents with us, and precious family photographs, books, mementos. As someone new to the Bay Area, I have never feared for wildfire in my life. Every time I had to pack these bags during the pandemic lockdown was a surreal experience. "I can't believe I'm doing this," I would say to myself, as I laid our bags, with my wedding photos next to the door.

From August to November we had to pack bags maybe six times. We only evacuated once, for one night, during a severe wind event, and there was only one weekend when the air quality was so bad because of raging wildfires in wine country that we couldn't go outside at all. But by far, the most terrifying day was the day that the sun never came out. The sky was a brilliant orange for a straight 24 hours, and it felt like the end of days.

September 9th I woke up around 7 a.m., and I took this photo of my bedroom window:

This is not photoshopped or altered in any way. We were under a red flag but the air quality had actually improved, despite the fact that it looked like we were in the middle of a fog out of a Stephen King short story. Though the morning went on, the sun never appeared. It felt like it was 5 a.m. all day. The sky was orange because "longer wavelength light (reds and oranges) are able to push through smoke particulates, whereas shorter wavelengths (blues and purples) are filtered out," according to a report I read on *Berkeleyside*, the local paper. Instagram was filled with East Bay orange shots. We went to bed that night saying to my son, "hopefully the sun will come out tomorrow."

The sun did reappear. I went outside to investigate. In our backyard, our lawn chair was covered in ash. The following day we drove into the city over the Bay Bridge. Halfway over the bridge, I could not see the city at all from behind the smoke.

Fog had turned into smoke.

The reason we decided to evacuate the night of the severe wind warning was because it was relatively easy for us to do so—even though we have a toddler and a dog—compared to other families with small children or elderly family members. As we drove to the hotel, I thought of all the people who live alone, wondering whether or not they should evacuate, or those sick with Covid-19 or tending to someone with the virus, those in the hospital, and the many homeless people in the Bay Area, out on the streets.

A night in a hotel was an interesting break in the routine. I sat in the bed, up with the sunrise, I looked over at my son sleeping on his mattress on the floor with our air purifier whirring. I read an article about how the Ohlone had managed the fires for 1,400 years by preventive burning, to combat drought, promote growth, and contain fires. In the same search, there was another article from the CDC about indigenous people being at higher risk for severe Covid-19 outcomes.

"By 1820, there seems to have been no more native people left in what today is Berkeley," Charles Wollenberg writes in his history of the city. The shell mounds were the only surviving evidence that a civilization had once thrived there. They, too, were picked apart and destroyed by settlers. "Some Bay Area cities used the materials unearthed to pave their streets," according to the *Earth Island Journal*, "literally lining them with the bones and ritual objects of Ohlone ancestors who had been interred within sacred burial grounds." Developers barreled on, moving the occupants of San Francisco's cemeteries in the same way, their tombstones ending up as foundations, sidewalks, and gutters. Though most records were destroyed in the 1906 earthquake, it is safe to assume there are bodies in Colma that were moved not once, not twice, but as many as three times.

The remains of the Ohlone and their sacred burial grounds haven't had the privilege to be transferred to a place like Colma. Though it was by no means a perfect system, there was at least the hope for reburial in a place that would be protective of the dead. The Ohlone and other native burials don't have anywhere to go. The remaining land that once belonged to them has been stolen. As the Ohlone have yet to be recognized by the federal government, they have little legal recourse.

"Solace and comfort can be found in the capacity of the ruins to survive the human tragedies they result from and record," Geoff Dyer writes in *The Missing of the Somme*, his book on the World War I memorials of France. He describes a fate worse than death, indeed worse than destruction or war, the destruction of memory itself. The Nazis, in their campaign in France, went to psychotic lengths to make sure nothing survived their rampage. After massacring entire villages, to make sure the place had been totally annihilated, "to make doubly sure, the cemetery was emptied of its dead who might have been a perpetual reminder that something existed in this place." Cemeteries would have been, like the shell mounds, the only indication that a culture, a town, a people, had lived there. So the Nazis emptied them of their dead and razed the whole graveyard. Entire towns disappeared, so that "no man could ever say there had been a village there."

THE SAND TRAP

Following a violent haunting and abduction in his home, Steve Freeling, a successful real estate developer played by Craig T. Nelson in the 1982 horror film *Poltergeist*, screams at his boss, "You moved the cemetery but you left the bodies, didn't you? You left the bodies and you moved only the headstones!" The idea that an entire community could be built atop a cemetery where thousands of bodies remain makes for a great scary movie plot. But it is the reality in many places in the United States, including at the Legion of Honor museum in San Francisco, where as many as 17,000 people remain, buried underneath the museum and the adjoining Lincoln Park Golf Course.

In 1993, the Legion of Honor was in need of a seismic retrofit, so the museum decided it would also take the opportunity to expand its galleries with an underground level. The renovation unearthed 750 bodies that had belonged to Golden Gate Cemetery, an active cemetery from 1869 to 1909. It wasn't exactly a surprise. Before the museum was planned, Golden Gate Cemetery was "moved" in 1909 as the city decided it needed a golf course. Lincoln Golf Course opened in 1917. The course you see today

was once the Potter's Field of Golden Gate Cemetery. On their website, the golf course describes their history: "What is presently the eighteenth fairway of the golf course was a burial ground, primarily for the city's Italian community. The area that now constitutes the first and thirteenth fairway was the Chinese section of the cemetery and the high terrain at the fifteenth fairway and thirteenth tee was a Serbian resting place."

Golden Gate Cemetery was founded in 1868, and the first interment took place in 1870. By the early 1900s, sadly, the cemetery had become an "eyesore," and the remains were ordered moved to Colma, with San Francisco's other cemeteries, in 1909. During the clearing of the cemetery to make way for the golf course, graves were desecrated. In a piece for the *San Francisco Morning Call* from December 16, 1908, the writer reported that the stone of one Mary Gribbich "had been broken and pried away, revealing the costly garments and the rings worn by the dead woman." Later, in 1921, as the Legion of Honor was being constructed, the vandalism continued. "I visited Lincoln Park," one man told the *Daily News*, "one large and two small skeletons were ripped out of one grave." The journalists reported just before Christmas in 1921, "many coffins—cut in half by the steel teeth of the excavating machines," and "a coffin sticking out of the sand bluff . . . one said that $35 had been found in one of the coffins, an expensive ring in another. And the skulls—sometimes students at the Affiliated colleges bought them." A lawyer took up the cause of the dead, claiming that it was illegal to use the land for any other purpose other than a cemetery. "I have pictures and facts showing that bodies were torn up as if they were so many stumps of trees," he told the *Daily News* on December 24, 1921, but his accusations of criminality went nowhere.

By 1911, the city claimed that all the graves had been moved to Colma. But the discovery of the 750 people in 1993 proves that this did not happen. "Surviving documents refer to the removal of fewer than 1,000 bodies," according to an archaeological paper published on the 1993 renovation, "and the contractors hired to move the burials appear to have removed only the headstones in many cases." According to existing documentation from Golden Gate Cemetery, 11,771 people were buried at Golden Gate in 1887 alone. Historians estimate as many as 18,000 people were buried there in total, meaning that as many as 17,000 could remain in the land that now holds the Legion of Honor and Lincoln Golf Course.

During the renovation, photographer Richard Barnes was able to visit and photograph the site, the subject of his exhibit and book *Still Rooms & Excavations*, published in 1997. The photographs

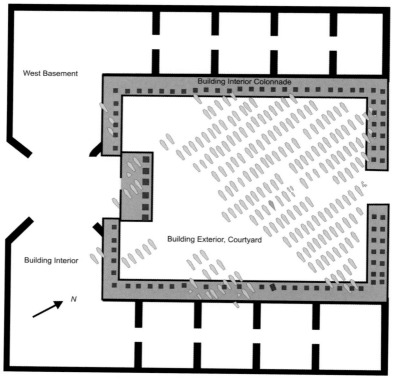

HISTORICAL ARCHAEOLOGY, THE SOCIETY FOR HISTORICAL ARCHAELOGY, VOLUME 35, NO. 2, SUMMER 2005; HEALTH AND DISEASE IN NINETEENTH-CENTURY SAN FRANCISCO: SKELETAL EVIDENCE FROM A FORGOTTEN CEMETERY, MICHELE R. BUZON, PHILLIP L. WALKER, FRANCINE DRAYER VERHAGEN, AND SUSAN L. KERR.

reveal the skeletons, still wearing buttons, their Levis, clutching rosaries. The archaeologists who studied the site noted that many of the remains appeared to be "amputated body parts, fetuses, preserved medical specimens, and other remains that appear to be hospital waste."

Barnes's capture of the excavated courtyard of the museum is stunning. At the top of one photograph, the Legion of Honor's white columns gleam resolutely, revealing a dark underbelly where workers clear burial sites. A smiling skull emerges from the ground. One skeleton, still in its coffin, is overlaid with plumbing for the building. Barnes's photographs also contain images of the museum exhibits inside, a severed marble head, an auditorium chairs shrouded in white sheets, the *Thinker* sculpture in the front courtyard wrapped in plastic, religious statues laying in pine boxes on the floor. The juxtaposition of the excavated remains and the objects inside the museum encapsulates the complex issues of human progress, the battle between the living and the dead, the story of San Francisco, and the history of many American cities.

In his introduction to the work, Barnes writes, "While working at the Legion of Honor I was struck by the apparent contradiction of a museum that both preserves and erases. . . . Here, the museum functions as a mausoleum, housing not only the objects of the dead but the dead themselves." Douglas Nickel, the Associate Curator of Photography at the San Francisco Museum of Museum of Modern Art, mentions that "Barnes points to the irony that, in its two waves of construction, the Palace excavations forced hundreds of San Francisco's original settlers to be exhumed from their graves and relocated, to make way for a museum dedicated to French art, and one replicating a building in France honoring French war dead at that."

Though archaeologists and historians pressed the city planner to continue the excavation of the site, the museum declined. According to a report from the *Los Angeles Times*, the San

Francisco Medical Examiner had the 750 remains reinterred at Skylawn Cemetery in San Mateo, and the artifacts were given to the City Museum.

Because of Covid-19 lockdown, the museum at the Legion of Honor was closed. I had seen Richard Barnes's photographs and was familiar with the museum through Hitchcock's *Vertigo*. Madeleine visits Carlotta Valdes's portrait at the Legion of Honor, where she brings a matching bouquet and sits in front of a bench in solemn reflection. I knew that Golden Gate Cemetery had been made into a golf course, but it was still shocking, driving through the entrance, to see that there were indeed several people, all men, outside, actively golfing. Near Lincoln Park Golf Course's main office there was a playground, so my husband and son decamped to play and I made my way up to the Legion of Honor, situated at Land's End. The view is spectacular—the museum and golf course looks directly over the bay, giving you a perfect vista of the Golden Gate Bridge and the city itself, downtown in the distance.

There were a few people parked in front of the Legion of Honor's fountain, and a few walking around, snapping photos or out with their dogs. There is a large sculpture, the same orange red as the Golden Gate Bridge, in the center of the fountain drive in front of the Legion of Honor by sculptor Mark di Suvero. Called *Pax Jerusalemme*, it resembles a large jack and was inspired by "ongoing conflicts in the Middle East," and by its proximity to the Holocaust Memorial. Holocaust Memorial? I had no idea there was a Holocaust Memorial at the Legion of Honor, but sure enough, directly to my right was a large sign, "Holocaust Memo-

rial," and a set of stairs. I made my way over, and was nearly knocked down by what I saw. A pile of white bodies, twisted in agony, behind a barbed wire fence, with one solitary male figure standing and looking out toward the Golden Gate Bridge. The sculpture was so intense and disturbing. I looked around to see if anyone else had noticed it. A few people sat near bench at the edge of the hill, oblivious or unconcerned.

As I stopped to read about the Holocaust Memorial, a man in a baseball cap in a golf cart drove by, whistling.

The memorial was designed by George Segal and dedicated in 1984. The figures are cast in bronze, painted shock white. According to the museum's website, several of the collapsed figures are symbolic: one resembles Christ, another Eve, holding an apple in her hand. The standing figure at the barbed wire is a reference to Margaret Bourke-White's 1945 photograph of the liberation of Buchenwald concentration camp. When I posted a photo of it on

Instagram, several people commented it was in "poor taste" and that it was "difficult to look at." The memorial has been vandalized several times, disturbingly, with swasitkas and red paint. It was recently restored by the museum in 2019, not because of vandalism, they claim, but rather due to the ravages of time and weather.

A plaque outside the memorial reads: "In Remembrance is the Secret of Redemption."

Unsettled, I walked over to the fountain. There was a single penny at the bottom. I crossed the street carefully, adjusting my face mask, and entered the sidewalk leading up to the courtyard of the Legion of Honor. There was a small plaque at the foot of the hedge. "The landscape of the Legion of Honor is proudly maintained by the San Francisco Recreation and Park Dept in partnership with dedicated Legion of Honor volunteers set December 1996." The year of this plaque felt like an odd coincidence. It seemed to say that the grounds were well looked after, which is undoubtedly true. But 1996 was the year the renovation work that had revealed the cemetery underneath the museum was wrapping up—Richard Barnes published his photographs of the excavation in 1997. And yet, there is no plaque, no memorial, no information anywhere on the grounds that indicates you are standing on top of a cemetery.

I made my way up to the building itself. The gates were padlocked, and Rodin's *Thinker* sat in the courtyard alone. It was a beautiful day, with bright blue skies and good visibility. There was a small glass pyramid, a skylight of sorts, that looked like the pyramid at the Louvre. The museum's insignia above its entrance is "Honneur et Patrie." Honor and Country. As I stopped to take photos, the sunlight blazed through the gates, making symmetrical lined shadows throughout the hallway.

Two sculptures, both by Anna Hyatt Huntington, guard the Legion of Honor. The first, on the left, is Joan of Arc, fitting, given the structure's French provenance. The other is El Cid, atop a gigantic stallion, its veins clearly visible and pulsating with life in the charge. Anna Hyatt Huntington survived tuberculosis and lived to be ninety-seven. With her husband, Archer M.

Huntington, she founded fourteen museums and four wildlife preserves. Her first Joan of Arc was made for New York. It was the first monument dedicated to a woman in the city.

I turned round the left corner of the museum to walk alongside the basement and to see the back of the building. On the immediate side there were several large trees, all planted by French officers on visits to the United States after World War I. Two men were finishing up on the putting green just beyond the trees. They both wore baseball hats but no masks. "Let's do it," one said the other. They got in their separate golf carts and drove off.

Halfway down the path, separating the golf course from the museum grounds is a replica of *Laocoön and His Sons*, a famous sculpture that resides at the Vatican, originally excavated in Rome in 1506. It portrays Laocoön and his two sons being attacked by sea serpents and is known as "the prototypical icon of human agony." The original sculpture was seized by Napoleon during his conquest of Italy in 1799 and returned after his fall in 1816. Its placement here was perplexing.

The light falling against the sculpture and the side wall of the museum was stunning. It was fairly quiet, aside from the hum of a generator at the back of the building. I rounded the corner and there was a tee, I'm not sure which hole, and two men stood chatting. There was a small freestanding restroom, and a park worker in a yellow vest eyed me as I took a turn looking at the back of the museum, its jutting half dome with busts of emperors, soldiers, and mythological figures.

On the other side there was a large parking lot, a view of the bay, and the rest of the golf course. A young man stood in front of a large stone slab with Japanese characters, taking photos. I waited for him to finish, then headed over. This monument was "erected to commemorate the arrival of the first Japanese naval ship Kanrin Maru in San Francisco Bay on 17 March 1860," a small plaque at its foot explained in English, "presented to the city of San Francisco by its sister city Osaka as a token of its sincere desire to

further strengthen the ties of friendship and goodwill . . . 17 May 1960."

As I was taking photos of the monument, a group of teen-age boys were exiting their respective cars heading out for their eighteen holes. I noticed that they were being responsible, and all wearing face masks, whereas most of the older male golfers that

day were not. The Bay Area had just been placed on our second extensive lockdown. Children could not go to school, people could not visit dying relatives in the hospital or in nursing homes, but these men could still play golf.

I pulled up my face mask as they walked by. "Hey," one boy nodded in my direction.

The amalgamation of many cultural signifiers left me a little light-headed: the French Legion of Honor, the desperate need for of all things a golf course in San Francisco, the second lockdown of the Bay Area, *Laocoön and His Sons*, the fact that nearly 17,000 bodies remained directly underneath us, the brutal Holocaust Memorial, El Cid, the Manifest Destiny of the bay itself, the Golden Gate Bridge and the Japanese monument, the pandemic, 350,000 dead Americans, the hope for "friendship and goodwill" in spite of nuclear war.

I walked back up the stairs and to the overlook, a large stone area above the golf course which looked over the city. Passing by the Holocaust Memorial, I noticed another plaque, for suffragist Frances E. Willard, who "became the first world organizer of women standing here she said: We are one world of tempted humanity." Standing here? Right here? And in the corner, there was another memorial, a bench for Russian veterans of World War II, dedicated November 11, 2000, and "donated by Bocci Memorials." Bocci Memorials is one of the oldest monument makers in Colma, a family business established in 1896. There are these plaques and memorials, but no memorial, no plaque, no sign for the occupants of the cemetery. The cemetery that still exists in this ground despite all attempts to erase it from memory.

There was a man standing at the point of the lookout, smoking. He very kindly moved aside so that I could take a few photos of the view. As I stepped forward I noticed there was a stand-alone obelisk underneath a large tree on the golf course, obviously a vestige of Golden Gate Cemetery. As I snapped as many photos as I could, the four teenage boys from the parking lot passed by, their golf clubs slung over their shoulders.

The obelisk, it turns out, is the Seaman's Memorial, erected by the Ladies' Seaman Friends Society. The location was obviously chosen for its fantastic view of the bay. The inscription reads: "A landmark of the seaman's last earthly port and resting-place in which he awaits the advent of The Great Pilot for his Eternal

Destiny." In 1891, the *San Francisco Examiner* hoped to bring the monument a little attention, as the cemetery was "wretched and forlorn." The reporters meet a gravedigger. "'Them's mariners,' said the gravedigger, who stood dreaming on his shovel, and flicking a curly dog with a coffin rope. 'They're put there so'st they can see the ships come in.'" The sad state of the cemetery is obvious from their description: "The wind rushes in from the sea and shakes the rattling branches of the scattered brush. Sometimes it overturns a tottering board or blows a broken paling from a falling fence. The place looks as if the gravedigger and his curly dog were the only visitors that ever came to visit it. Except the wind. That is always there." And now, golfers.

I thanked the smoking man for stepping aside for me and made my way down the main drive back toward the golf course office and the playground to rejoin my husband and son. It was not without a certain amount of anxiety as I strode down the golf course, covering my head in my hands to protect myself from soaring balls.

As I walked by one hole, in the distance, in the middle of the fairway, I saw what looked like a hollowed-out mausoleum in between some trees. It had an arched entry way and back stone wall, but it was empty, a ruin. I imagined the occupants had been removed and over time the structure had degraded. I wanted to get closer, but it was an active golf course and I could see there was a group teeing off in the distance. I tried to get as close as I could with my camera.

It is, in fact, not a mausoleum, but all that remains of Land's End Chinese Cemetery. Long before World War II and the Chinese Revolution, it had been the practice of Chinese immigrants to be buried here in San Francisco, and when their remains had decomposed, their bones would be sent back to China for burial with their ancestors. This structure is the marker for this section that eventually became a part of Golden Gate Cemetery. Now it is an obstacle for golfers, a trap made in the sands of time and forgetting.

EPILOGUE

I had intended to write about Covid-19 and what mass death does to our already rocky relationship with death to conclude this book, but history won't stop happening. I've had to update the Covid-19 death toll number several times over the course of writing this manuscript. Current events keep coming. The news cycle is so relentless that it makes it feel like months, even years pass between a single day. This is the work of the pandemic. Our minds cannot shoulder the enormous burden of loss on such a mass scale, much less begin to process it.

I believe that a close relationship with our death creates a better life. But the pandemic annihilates the opportunity for a "good death." Families can not be present with their loved ones in the hospital at the time of death. Morgues are overflowing. Mass burials are necessary. People are watching funerals for their family members on Zoom. In her piece about the pandemic in the *London Review of Books*, Jacqueline Rose writes that death on this mass scale has "made it feel to many for the first time that death is something of which a person—the one dying, and those closest to her or him—can be robbed."

SAN FRANCISCO HISTORY CENTER, SAN FRANCISCO PUBLIC LIBRARY

In the same piece, Rose relays the advice of a palliative care doctor. She says that when "statistics throw me off balance," she tries to "keep things as small as I can." She doesn't explain how she does this, but I imagine she means she focuses on each patient, and what gesture or task she can complete to restore that person's dignity. We can apply the idea of "keeping things small" in our own lives. The Colma necropolis is a staggering place to grapple with psychically. But if you can distill it down to a single grave, a single person, it brings out the humanity of the place. I keep things small by taking pictures, by looking for those moments of light or beauty that help me to see the cemetery not only as a landscape but as individual portraits.

Certainly, some denial of death is necessary to forging ahead, both physically and emotionally. The cemeteries of San Francisco were moved to Colma to make way for the living, for progress, for life. The sacred burial grounds of the first people of this country are moved to make way for corporate office buildings. When we lose the dead, we lose their stories. We push death to the farthest corners of our minds, in service of "progress," the same concept the created the city of San Francisco: of Manifest Destiny, of control of the port, of the land—the Gold Rush. Today we call it capitalism. "The destiny of one's race meant the holocaust of another," writes Gray Brechin in *Imperial San Francisco*. "'Whole tribes and nations of picturesque men and women have vanished before this great 'Star of Empire.'" Essential workers endanger themselves in the service of the economy. Hispanic, Latinx and BIPOC are almost three times as likely to die from Covid-19 than white people.

In a lengthy *New Yorker* piece about the pandemic, Lawrence Wright interviews several doctors and infectious disease experts who are reminded of other patients who came into the hospital horribly sick not so long ago. "Almost all of them died," one remembers, as the hospital staff struggled to understand what was happening. They were the first AIDS patients. Those who lost loved ones to AIDS know all too well what happens when a government decides which citizens are worth protecting.

The night before their 2021 inauguration, President Joe Biden and Vice President Kamala Harris gathered with their spouses to light the Lincoln Memorial Reflecting Pool in remembrance of those who have died from Covid-19. It's a good start.

When workers were clearing Golden Gate Cemetery in the early 1900s for the creation of the Lincoln Park Golf Course, as photographer Richard Barnes recounted to *SF Weekly*, they "plowed through burial sites, and plumbers laid pipes right through bodies and skeletons. They threw headstones off the cliff into the ocean." Those tombstones washed up on Ocean Beach, and some were used to reinforce the sea wall on the beach. When high winds blow, usually in the spring, some of the tombstones emerge from the sand, at the intersection of the Great Highway and Rivera Street.

John Martini, a National Park Service ranger, said that the winds also reveal shipwrecks and other interesting things on the beach, but then the winds cover the tombstones up again. "They turned up some years ago in about the same place," he told *SF Gate* in 2012. "There was a big fuss, and then they were covered up again. How soon we forget."

It was not spring when we drove out to Ocean Beach, so I wasn't sure what to expect. It was a bright and sunny day in early December. The beach was large, much larger than the bay beaches we had visited. I had to remind myself that this was different, this is the ocean. There were a few people out on the beach with their dogs, and no one was in the water. We had driven and parked at the exact intersection where the tombstones were supposed to be visible. My husband and son played with a wooden airplane while I walked up and down the sea wall, looking for any evidence of gravestones.

There were large sand dunes. Probably the tombstones were underneath, but completely covered. I walked up one large dune only to find a couple engaged in a serious-looking conversation. I apologized for the interruption as they pulled up their face masks.

I doubled back to my husband and son.

"Any luck?" he asked.

I shook my head but kept looking. I found the skeleton of a crab, and a completely detached wing of a bird, with beautiful purple gray feathers, but no stones.

I thought of asking one of the people on the beach if they had seen any tombstones, but it seemed like an odd thing to do, and I decided against it.

The ocean was beautiful. Living in New York, because we didn't own a car, we rarely went to the beach. In the Bay Area, especially in the East Bay, all I need to do is go for a walk to be reminded of our proximity to the water.

We decided to pack it in. As my family got our things together, I wandered over to take a few photographs of the elevated sidewalk,

its underside covered in bright graffiti. Next to the sand, it made for an interesting picture. Just below the stairs, there was a large rock.

I stepped down to get closer and brushed the sand away with my hand. I thought about trying to lift it but it was enormous. There wasn't any text visible, but the corners were indented, and lined, like a border. I took a few photos.

My husband noticed what I was doing and said, hopefully, "Yeah?"

I shrugged, smiling up at him. "Who knows?"

ACKNOWLEDGMENTS

To Danae at Greek Orthodox Memorial Park and to Jeff Lindeman and Kristie Ly at Mountain View Cemetery, thank you so much for your time. Thank you to David Gallagher at Outside Lands. At Globe Pequot, many thanks to Amy Lyons, my production editor Meredith Dias, and proofreader Susan Barnett, for holding me accountable. To my agent, Katelyn Detweiler—thank you for your guidance and good faith.

Thank you to my family: Mom, Rob, and Nick, to Howard and Helen, and to my husband Graham, for all your support and encouragement, and especially to Graham who took on more caregiving responsibilities so that I could work. To my therapist: your support and guidance helps me tremendously. I want to thank Boris for the work. Though we survived 2020, many people did not. May their memory be a blessing. To my son Roman—thank you for reminding me that in thinking about the past, it is important to consider the future.

NOTES AND SOURCES

PART I: SAN FRANCISCO: THE FAILED STAR

Introduction
City of Souls, Michael Svanevik and Shirley Burgett, 1995.

The Mission
Berkeley: A City in History, Charles Wollenberg, 2008.

"City Planner Report: Location, Regulation, and Removal of Cemeteries in the City and County of San Francisco," William A. Proctor, 1950.

"To Die One's Own Death," Jacqueline Rose, *New York Review of Books*, November 19, 2020.

"Why Are There So Many Dead People in Colma? And So Few in San Francisco?" Jon Brooks, KQED, October 26, 2017.

Imperial San Francisco, Gray Brechin, 1999.

The Glorious Dead
Imperial San Francisco, Gray Brechin, 1999.

The Missing of the Somme, Geoff Dyer, 1994.

"Modoc War," Stephen R. Mark, *Oregon Encyclopedia*.

"Four More Heads for the Indian Trophy Room," Robert Aquinas McNally, *Indian Country Today*, September 13, 2018.

Pauline Cushman. National Park Service. Golden Gate National Recreation Area, nps.gov/people/paulinecushman.htm.

This Particular Death Was Not Inevitable
Close to the Knives, David Wojnarowicz, 1991.

"The Rage and Tenderness of David Wojnarowicz's Art." Christine Smallwood, *New York Times* Magazine, September 7, 2018.

PART II: DEATH & CO.: PORTRAITS OF COLMA

City of Souls, Michael Svanevik and Shirley Burgett, 1995.

Colma: Images of America, Michael Smookler, 2007.

"Abigail Folger: The Lesser-Known Victim of the Tate Murders," Gina DiMuro, *All That's Interesting*, November 28, 2018.

Stories in Stone, Douglas Keister, 2004.

California Grizzly Bear, Valley Center History Museum, vchistory.org/exhibits/grizzly-bear.

Curtains, Tom Jokinen, 2010.

"Inmate to Face Trial in 1978 Killings of Teens Near Barstow," Sandra Murillo, *Los Angeles Times*, March 23, 2004.

"Why Are There So Many Dead People in Colma? And So Few in San Francisco?" Jon Brooks, KQED, October 26, 2017.

"Biographies of People at Poson—One of America's Concentration Camps." Ishida, George S. S/Sgt. (14-3-A) MIS. 441st CIC area 25 Yokohama (website).

Impounded, Linda Gordon and Gary Y. Okhiro, eds., 2008.

"City Planner Report: Location, Regulation, and Removal of Cemeteries in the City and County of San Francisco," William A. Proctor, 1950.

"Grave Sighting: Wyatt Earp." Stacy Conradt, *Mental Floss*, October 17, 2016.

PART III: CONTRA COSTA: THE EAST BAY

Library of Souls
Julia Morgan: Architect of Beauty, Mark Anthony Wilson, 2007.

The View from Here
On the Wintermute mausoleum: "For Sale in Oakland: 1 Room, Great View, Quiet Neighborhood, $250,000." Patricia Lee Brown, *The New York Times*, October 30, 2003.

For more on Ghirardelli, Miller, Colton, and Ryer monuments: Lives of the Dead: Mountain View Cemetery in Oakland, Michael Culbruno, mountainviewpeople.blogspot.com.

Ghirardelli and Merritt Mausoleums: Douglas Keister, mausoleums.com.

On Gwin mausoleum: *Imperial San Francisco*, Gray Brechin, 1999.

"Yesterday's Crimes: The Black Dahlia Lies in Oakland." Bob Calhoun. *SF Weekly*. July 3, 2017.

Exclusive Use

"On the Wrong Side of the Fence: Racial Segregation in American Cemeteries," Angelika Krüger-Kahloula, *History & Memory in African-American Culture*, 1994.

Long vs. Mountain View Cemetery Association, 1955.

Jones vs. Alfred H. Mayer, 1968.

The Second Gold Rush, Marilynn S. Johnson, 1993.

"Jonestown Memorial," *Atlas Obscura*, atlasobscura.com/places/jonestown-memorial.

"The Demographics of Jonestown," Rebecca Moore, *Alternative Considerations of Jonestown & People's Temple*, San Diego State University.

Oya, Santeria Church of the Orishas, santeriachurch.org/the-orishas/oya.

"The Chaos of Alamont and the Murder of Meredith Hunter," Sasha Frere-Jones, *The New Yorker*, March 28, 2019.

"Police: Hells Angel Sparked Minneapolis Riots after George Floyd's Death." Associated Press, July 28, 2020.

"Child Was Their 'Whole Life' So Couple Joined Him in Death," *Arizona Daily Star*, June 28, 1984.

"Earl Hines," Hal Smith, The San Francisco Traditional Jazz Foundation Collection, The Charles N. Huggins Project, Stanford University.

Part IV: What Remains

The Gutter
San Francisco Cemeteries, John W. Blackett, http://www.sanfranciscocemeteries.com.

Garden of Innocence
"145-year-old casket with preserved toddler found beneath San Francisco home," Joseph Serna, The *Los Angeles Times*, May 26, 2016.

City of Souls, Michael Svanevik and Shirley Burgett, 1995.

"Mystery Solved: Remains of Girl in Forgotten Casket Was Daughter of Prominent San Francisco Family," Joseph Serna, *Los Angeles Times*, May 10, 2017.

Suddenly San Francisco, Charles Lockwood, 1978.

"Remains of the Day: A Native American Burial Discovered in San Francisco Is Shrouded in a Fog of Acrimony," Peter W. Colby, Anthropology Now, April 26, 2016.

"Bones of Discontent—Andrew Galvan Carves a Unique, Controversial Role in Relocating Native American Skeletons," Ron Russell, *SF Weekly*, November 21, 2007.

"West Berkeley Shellmound Is Now Considered one of the U.S.'s 11 Most Endangered Historic Places," Frances Dinkelspiel, Berkeleyside, September 25, 2020.

"Paved Over Ohlone Shellmound Site in Berkeley Listed as Endangered Historic Place," Fiona McLeod, *Earth Island Journal*, September 25, 2020.

"Court rules development can proceed on West Berkeley Shellmound," Lauren Good, *The Daily Californian*, April 27, 2021.

Berkeley: A City in History, Charles Wollenberg, 2008.

The Missing of the Somme, Geoff Dyer, 1994.

The Sand Trap

News reports on the relocation of Golden Gate Cemetery from the Golden Gate Cemetery entry on San Francisco Cemeteries, San Francisco Cemeteries, John W. Blackett, http://www.sanfranciscocemeteries.com.

Still Rooms & Excavations, Richard Barnes, 1997.

Epilogue

"To Die One's Own Death," Jacqueline Rose. *The New York Review of Books*. November 19, 2020.

Imperial San Francisco, Gray Brechin, 1999.

"The Plague Year," Lawrence Wright, *The New Yorker*, December 28, 2020.

"Why Are There So Many Dead People in Colma? And So Few in San Francisco?" Jon Brooks. KQED. October 26, 2017.

"Tombstones from Long Ago Surface on S.F. Beach," Carl Nolte, *SFGate*, June 8, 2012.

ABOUT THE AUTHOR

Jessica Ferri is the author of *Silent Cities New York*. Her work has been published by the *Los Angeles Times*, NPR, *The Economist*, the *Daily Beast*, and more. She lives in Northern California.